★

THE
GREAT
DISSENTER
John Marshall Harlan
1833-1911

Frank B. Latham

★

THE
GREAT
DISSENTER

John Marshall Harlan
1833 ★ 1911

COWLES BOOK COMPANY, INC. ★ New York

for Lucille, Linda, and Bob

SBN 402-14141-5

Library of Congress Catalog Card Number 79-104353

Cowles Book Company, Inc.
A subsidiary of Cowles Communications, Inc.

Published simultaneously in Canada by
  General Publishing Company, Ltd.
    30 Lesmill Road, Don Mills, Toronto, Ontario

Printed in the United States of America

First Edition

Contents

★
Foreword

A few years back, a magazine editor, aware of my favorite form of self-expression, asked me for a set of nine limericks about the then sitting Justices of the Supreme Court. The toughest of the lot for me to fix in five lines of verse was a gentle and genial friend of mine whose slant toward the law of the Constitution could scarcely have been more at odds with my own. Someone once called him "Frankfurter without the mustard." What I wrote went like this:

> John M. Harlan would valiantly save
> A high court which he sees misbehave;
>   Unrestrained is his plaint:
>   "We must use self-restraint"—
> While his grandfather turns in his grave.

"Justice Harlan's grandfather, eh—who in hell was he?" asked every single non-lawyer and nine out of every ten lawyers who reported to me that they had read my limericks. Who indeed? John Marshall Harlan, named for "the great Chief Justice" and eventually followed to the Supreme Court by his namesake and grandson, has been, for going on a century now, the least well known, the most neglected by alleged legal scholars, of the handful of genuine judicial giants whose genius has blessed our highest bench.

Harlan the First sat up there for a little less than thirty-four years, a term of service topped to date only by Justice Stephen J. Field and Chief Justice John Marshall. He wrote more than eleven hundred opinions—perhaps the Court's record, unless Justice William O. Douglas has recently inched ahead—of which three hundred odd were dissents. Frank Latham, to whose brand-new book these remarks are a sort of prefatory fanfare, is wholly justified in hailing Harlan—instead of Holmes, the household hero from Olympus—as "the Great Dissenter."

And not just by quantitative count. Harlan's often solo blasts—in behalf of civil liberties and civil rights and against farfetched use of phrases out of the Constitution to kill laws, at whatever level, that regulated business or taxed wealth—were for the most part miles ahead of Holmes, both chronologically and philosophically.

It was almost a century ago that this ex-slaveholder and ardent Constitutionalist from Kentucky dissented alone

against the decision of eight brethren—whose counter-
parts Messieurs Mitchell, Nixon, and Thurmond would
dearly love to find for the Court today—that the Civil
Rights Act of 1875 was unconstitutional. Eloquent,
angry, and alone again, Harlan would have no truck a
few years later with his fellows' judicial injection into the
Constitution of the trite but inaccurate phrase "separate
but equal." (Inaccurate? Try it on your nearest legal quiz
kid. The Louisiana law upheld in *Plessy* v. *Ferguson*—
under a doctrine not disowned until the Warren Court
did so almost six decades later—called for "equal but
separate" accommodations for blacks and whites.) Snarled
Harlan, more prophetically than accurately: "Our Constitution is color-blind."

Even more remarkably prophetic and equally lonely
was Harlan's insistence (in a case called *Hurtado* v.
California) that the "due process" clause of the Fourteenth Amendment was intended to carry over against
state governments the civil liberties protected against
federal infringement by the Bill of Rights. It was for this
that Justice Frankfurter, when the same question came
up during the 1940s, branded Harlan "an eccentric exception" among past judges—even though that presumably made the four contemporary fellow Justices who
dissented from Frankfurter's view "eccentric," too. And,
indeed, decisions of this century, gradually absorbing the
guarantees of the Bill of Rights into the Fourteenth
Amendment, both before and more speedily since Frank-

furter's death, may yet make him, not Harlan, the eccentric exception in the eye of history.

Not that all Harlan's multitude of major dissents were one-man jobs. He was one of a quartet who inveighed in vain against the Court's veto of the Democratic-Populist income tax in the 1890s, thus forcing, too long after, the passage of the Sixteenth Amendment. And though Holmes's elegant little dissent in the *Lochner* case (killing a maximum-hour law) is widely known and quoted—"the Fourteenth Amendment does not enact Mr. Herbert Spencer's Social Statics" and "general propositions do not decide concrete cases"—almost no one, even among lawyers, is aware that it was the devastating separate dissent by Harlan, whose term overlapped Holmes's, that won over two more Justices to join his opinion, not Holmes's, so that they almost upset the unholy five-to-four holding.

But I must steal no more of Mr. Latham's thunder, even though I mean only to add a little preliminary lightning as a kind of come-on. Just a couple of further comments:

Maybe ten or twelve years ago, I wrote a magazine article choosing what I called an all-time all-American Supreme Court. Toward the eighth and ninth members, the going got tough. But well before that, I had put on my list of nine the only all-timer whose service spanned two centuries. That is one reason I welcome, at too long last, this first—so far as I know—book-length biography of the elder Justice John Marshall Harlan even though the book be small. What lunkheads legal historians must be to leave so formidable a figure uncelebrated so long.

A second reason why I welcome this work of Frank Latham's is my belief, since way back, that lawyers are lousy writers, especially when they write about lawyers and law. One of the best biographies of a Supreme Court member ever written is political scientist Don Morgan's job on Justice William Johnson, first of all the great dissenters. Most widely read of such biographies, I dare say, was Catherine Bowen's Book-of-the-Month on Holmes. Mrs. Bowen is no lawyer.

Neither, thank God, is Mr. Latham. His book is brightly written, easily read, and fortunately free, perforce, of legalistic logorrhea. I commend it to lawyers as well as laymen and will doubtless continue to do so even after my professorial friend, Alan Westin, to whom Mr. Latham makes generous gestures, completes the more am-bitious Harlan biography on which he is at work.

After these well-earned words of welcome and warmth for him and his book, maybe Mr. Latham will not mind if I carp just once in conclusion. He is so up-to-date that he mentions a case called *Benton* v. *Maryland* in which the decision was handed down on the Warren Court's final day, June 23, 1969. He mentions it because this *Benton* decision added one more case-worth of weight to the prophetic validity of Harlan the First's lone and "eccentric" dissent against the *Hurtado* holding, eighty-five years before. Don't you think Mr. Latham might have mentioned, too, as a kicker, that the author of the two-man turn-the-clock-back dissent in the *Benton* case was none other than Justice John Marshall Harlan the Second?

Fred Rodell
Professor of Law
Yale University

★
Introduction

In 1865, soon after the end of the American Civil War, the Thirteenth Amendment to the Constitution freed the Negro from bondage. Three years later the Fourteenth Amendment declared him a citizen, entitled to "the equal protection of the laws." In 1870 the Fifteenth Amendment gave him the right to vote. But subsequent decisions by the Supreme Court of the United States denied to the Negro rights granted in these amendments. The freedman was still not a free man.

In 1883, in the *Civil Rights Cases*, the Supreme Court declared unconstitutional the Civil Rights Act of 1875, which required for all races "the full and equal enjoyment of accommodations in inns, theaters . . . and public conveyances." Then, in 1896, in the case *Plessy* v. *Ferguson*, the Court upheld a Louisiana law requiring all railroads to provide "equal but separate accommodations for the white and colored races."

For more than fifty years after the *Plessy* decision the Southern states were free, in fact were encouraged, to pass a wide range of laws denying blacks equality, even though some whites wanted to give them equal treatment.

The lone dissenter in the *Civil Rights* and *Plessy* cases was Justice John Marshall Harlan. His dissent in *Plessy* v. *Ferguson* proved to be a chilling and accurate prediction of things to come in the nation's black ghettos: "In my opinion, the judgment this day rendered will, in time, prove quite as pernicious as the decision made by this tribunal in the Dred Scott case [which all but made the Civil War inevitable]. . . . The destinies of the two races in this country are indissolubly linked together and the interests of both require that the common government of all not permit the seeds of race hate to be planted under the sanction of law."

Finally the Court caught up with Harlan's vision, but it was later than anyone thought—too late to head off much racial strife. In 1954, in the case of *Brown* v. *Board of Education,* the Court unanimously knocked out segregation in public education. "We conclude," said Chief Justice Earl Warren, "that in the field of public education the doctrine of 'separate but equal' has no place. Separate educational facilities are inherently unequal." Ten years later the Court, again unanimously, upheld that section of the Civil Rights Act of 1964 requiring desegregation of public accommodations. The 1964 act was the most sweeping civil rights measure since the ill-fated act of 1875.

John Marshall Harlan's lone voice had become the voice of a unanimous Court; his dissents had become the law of the land.

Strangely this man who fought alone for Negro rights and common sense in race relations was an ex-slaveholder from Kentucky who once denounced Lincoln's Emancipation Proclamation as "unconstitutional and null and void." He said he would oppose the Thirteenth Amendment "if there were not a dozen slaves in the state of Kentucky," and he defiantly announced that he had not freed his slaves until forced to do so by law. He condemned the Fourteenth Amendment and warned that the Republican party was intending to deny the vote "to almost the entire white population" of the South while giving it to the Negro.

Later, however, the flickering torches of night-riding, anti-Negro terrorists convinced Harlan that Republican policies had been correct and that Congress had to act to defend Negro rights and to rebuild a war-torn nation. Swinging over to the Republican party, Harlan became its candidate for governor of Kentucky in 1871. During this campaign he had the courage to change his mind in public. He didn't excuse himself or try to explain away his proslavery past. He called slavery "the most perfect despotism that ever existed on this earth," and when hecklers read his anti-Negro, proslavery speeches to him, Harlan replied: "Let it be said that I am right rather than consistent."

His nomination as an associate justice of the Supreme Court aroused the opposition of those still suspicious of his proslavery past. But when this towering, jovial, tobacco-chewing judge took his place on the bench, he became a steadfast, often solitary defender not only of Negro civil rights, but of every citizen's right to a fair trial and the blessings of liberty under the Constitution.

1

★

James Harlan and Son

In Kentucky in the year of 1833, it was the best of times or the worst of times—depending on the point of view. It was the best of times to James Harlan, a well-to-do lawyer and slave owner of Harlan Station, Boyle County. Harlan was a close friend of Henry Clay, who was a leader of the Whig party, which believed in a national bank and internal improvements (highways, canals, and railroads) to bind the states into a strong national government. Clay and Harlan opposed the "tyranny" of "King" Andrew Jackson, then president of the United States. But both men applauded Jackson's firm stand against John C. Calhoun of South Carolina, who argued that each state in the Federal Union had the right to defy any law of Congress that it felt was harmful to its interests. Lifting his glass at a formal dinner, Jackson had glared at Calhoun

1

and offered this toast: "The Federal Union, it must be preserved!"

Later, Jackson threatened to use troops and warships against South Carolina and "to hang John Calhoun" when that state asserted the right to nullify an act of Congress and to secede from the Union. South Carolina objected to a tariff law that, by levying high duties on foreign products, raised the prices on certain products that Southerners wanted to buy. Eventually, Henry Clay worked out a compromise tariff that satisfied both Calhoun and Jackson, ending the quarrel.

On June 1, 1833, a son was born to James and Eliza Davenport Harlan. The boy was named for John Marshall, whose decisions as Chief Justice of the Supreme Court from 1801 to 1835 had greatly strengthened the national government. At his son's birth James Harlan looked out on a world that suited him. The young United States was strong and growing more prosperous each year. In spite of the wild ranting of antislavery Northerners led by abolitionist William Lloyd Garrison, slavery was protected by the Constitution of the United States. And Congress had passed a fugitive slave law to force the return of runaway slaves to their masters.

To young Cassius Marcellus Clay, a cousin of Henry Clay, 1833 was the worst of times. He had returned from a year of study at Yale College in New Haven, Connecticut, where he had heard William Lloyd Garrison denounce slavery. "On this subject," said Garrison, "I do

not wish to think or speak or write with moderation. . . .
I will not excuse—I will not retreat a single inch—and I
will be heard!" In reply to the Southern argument that
cotton could not be raised without slave labor, Garrison
stubbornly wrote, "Then let's not raise any more cotton,
if it has to be grown by a race in bondage!"

Young Cassius Clay also read Garrison's paper, the
Liberator, which carried the statement: "No Union with
slaveholders. The United States Constitution is a cov-
enant with death and an agreement with hell."

Back home at White Hall, his father's plantation in
Madison County, Cassius Clay looked at the sweating
slaves and reached a shattering decision. He resolved to
free his slaves and become an antislavery crusader—
practically a man alone in that part of Kentucky.

Although this is the story of John Marshall Harlan,
Cassius Clay is part of the story because his, as well as
Harlan's, words and deeds show so clearly how the clash
over slavery divided both the hearts and minds of men of
goodwill.

John Marshall Harlan, a cultured Southern gentleman
and slave owner, and Cassius Marcellus Clay, a rough-
and-tumble foe of slavery who carried two pistols and a
bowie knife when he faced proslavery crowds, both wound
up on the same side during the Civil War. They stood for
the Union—but with a difference. As the organizer and
commander of the Tenth Kentucky Volunteer Infantry
Regiment, Harlan told his troops that he would quit and

lead them into the Confederate army if Lincoln and the Radical Republicans in Washington tried to abolish slavery. Clay was commissioned as a brigadier general in the Union army, but he refused to fight until Lincoln took steps to free the slaves. Wearing his uniform, Clay had faced a crowd at Odd Fellows Hall in Washington on August 13, 1862, and shouted: "Never, so help me God, will I draw my sword to keep the chains upon another fellow being!"

2
★
Quiet Before the Storm

While he was growing up, John Marshall Harlan lived a quiet, uneventful life in a comfortable mansion staffed with Negro slaves. He was tutored at home and often went with his father and Henry Clay to Whig political rallies. Standing among crowds at picnic grounds lit by flaring torches, young Harlan heard his father and Clay defend a strong national government and uphold the Constitution as the supreme law of the land.

James Harlan, who had once served as state attorney general of Kentucky, was elected to the U.S. House of Representatives in 1835. When his second two-year term in Congress ended, Harlan resumed the practice of law. He later was elected to the Kentucky legislature. There, he heard the fiery Cassius Clay denounce slavery.

Young Cassius Clay's life on his father's plantation had

been comfortable but far from quiet and uneventful. A hot-tempered youth, he had, all in one day, quarreled violently with his mother and gotten into fist fights with his tutor and a slave companion. A few years later, on the day before his wedding, Clay had used his cane on a rival for the lady's hand in the streets of Louisville. Clay was elected to the legislature from Madison County in 1835 and 1837. Then he moved to Lexington and was elected to the legislature from Fayette County in 1840.

In 1842, against the advice of his cousin Henry Clay, Cassius ran for a seat in the legislature on an out-and-out antislavery platform and lost. Henry Clay insisted that he was "no friend of slavery," but he contended that it was "better that slaves should remain slaves than be set loose as free men among us." He did, however, serve as president of the American Colonization Society, which in thirty years managed to set free and send more than 6,000 slaves to its African colony of Liberia. James Harlan, and later his son, favored Clay's effort to rid the nation of slavery eventually.

Cassius Clay scoffed at the American Colonization Society's attempt to solve the slavery problem. He pointed out that many more blacks were born each year than could possibly be sent to Liberia in thirty years. Boldly, Cassius Clay insisted on gradual emancipation with each state paying slaveholders for their freed slaves. This proposal enraged many members of the American Colonization Society. They did not want free Negroes living in the

South because their presence might encourage slaves to run away or even rebel against their owners.

Stepping up his antislavery crusade, Cassius Clay founded a newspaper in Lexington called the *True American*. Since it was published in one of the state's largest slaveholding areas and was edited by a man born in Kentucky, the *True American* proved to be a most bothersome foe of slavery. Clay fortified his newspaper office with two cannons, plus rifles, lances, and a keg of gunpowder, which he could touch off from the outside to blow up the office and any invaders. These precautions were not just playacting or bluff. Earlier, Clay had fought one duel with a proslavery man in which no blood was spilled. But later he mutilated another assailant with a bowie knife. After first dismissing Clay as the "Yale-schoolboy emancipationist," prominent proslavery citizens of Lexington decided that action had to be taken against him. In August, 1845, while Clay was ill, a crowd broke into his office, boxed up all the equipment, and shipped it across the Ohio River to Cincinnati. After his recovery Clay stubbornly opened a new office and continued to publish his paper both in Cincinnati and Louisville.

While Cassius Clay was writing, speaking, and fending off opponents, young John Marshall Harlan was learning the fundamentals of Presbyterianism at Centre College in Danville, Kentucky.

In 1850, Harlan's final year at Centre College, Cassius Clay engaged in a near-fatal "debate" with a proslavery man, Cyrus Turner. Stabbed over the heart by Turner, Clay plunged his bowie knife into his assailant's abdomen. The *Lexington Observer and Reporter* said that Clay was dead, but in its next issue, it said: "Mr. Clay still lives, but his adversary, Mr. Turner, lingered until about 12 o'clock on Saturday night when he expired."

The indomitable Clay was soon on the speaker's platform again. "Would you help a runaway slave?" shouted a heckler. "That would depend on which way he was running," replied Clay.

3
★
The Young Giant

Deciding to follow his father's profession, John Harlan studied law at Transylvania University, "the Harvard of the West," in Lexington, Kentucky. At the age of twenty he was admitted to the bar and began to practice law in his father's office in Frankfort, the capital of Kentucky.

Soon young Harlan was active in the Whig party, which unfortunately was sinking to its death. Badly split by the slavery issue, the party made the mistake of trying to ignore the problem. In 1852, the Whig presidential candidate was Winfield Scott, a good soldier but a totally inept politician. The Democrats had no trouble winning with a second-rate man, Franklin Pierce. At a time when the nation needed a strong president, neither party seemed able or willing to provide such a man. The final blow was dealt the Whigs when Democratic Senator Stephen

A. Douglas brought out his bill to divide the Nebraska Territory into two territories—Kansas and Nebraska. Douglas also proposed to settle the heated question of slavery in the territories with the doctrine of "popular sovereignty"—or "squatter sovereignty." This meant that the people of Kansas and Nebraska would vote on whether to have slavery or not. Passage by Congress of the Kansas-Nebraska Act in 1854 resulted in the repeal of the Missouri Compromise of 1820, which banned slavery in the upper Missouri Valley. For the first time in the nation's history, territory once closed to slavery had been opened to it again. This fact infuriated antislavery Northerners, both Democrats and Whigs. Many of them deserted their parties and joined the new Republican party. Abraham Lincoln, who had served one undistinguished term in Congress as a Whig representative from Illinois, made a name for himself by speaking against Douglas and the Kansas-Nebraska Act.

Buffeted and confused by the Kansas-Nebraska uproar, some of the Kentucky Whigs drifted into the Democratic party. But a majority of the Whigs in the state made a last desperate effort to win power by working with the new Native American party. Critics called it the Know-Nothing party because members answered all questions regarding their activities with: "I know nothing about it." The Know-Nothings took an oath to vote only for "natives" (people born in America) , and to demand that immigrants must live here twenty-one years before they could vote. The party also strongly opposed the influence of the Catholic church.

The Know-Nothings' list of hates appealed to a wide range of people and made the party a power in American politics for several years. In 1854 at least seventy-five congressmen were elected with Know-Nothing support. In 1855 the party elected governors in nine states.

In Kentucky, the Whig-American (Know-Nothing) alliance got its first test in the 1855 elections. James Harlan was fighting for reelection as attorney general, and his son campaigned vigorously for him. A handsome, six-foot-two-inch redhead with a powerful but pleasant voice, John Harlan quickly won a reputation as a skilled campaigner. Carrying his possessions in two saddle bags, Harlan rode from town to town on horseback and skillfully debated Democratic veterans twice his age. The *Frankfort Commonwealth* reported party leaders as saying that one of his speeches was "the clearest and ablest exposition of American principles" ever heard in their town. These "American principles" involved charges that the immigrants were paupers and criminals, that they "come here almost invariably prejudiced against the institution of slavery," that the "rulers of the Catholic world claim or seek political supremacy in America," and that the Germans were out to make "war against religion and the rights of property."

No one knows how seriously John Harlan took these arguments, but he had been educated at Centre, a strict Presbyterian school that took a dim view of Catholicism. He was also an officer in the Younger Brothers of Temperance Society, which looked with distaste and suspicion on the beer-drinking immigrants.

At the end of the 1855 campaign, the *Lexington Observer and Reporter* said that Harlan's speeches had "left an impression that will not be effaced for a long time." Harlan's spirits were lifted by this praise and by the clean-sweep victory of the Whig-Americans. They won every state office from the governorship on down. Harlan was disturbed, however, by the "Bloody Monday" riots in Louisville on August 6. The Whig-Americans were accused of attacks upon Democrats that resulted in the deaths of several people.

Another blow was dealt the Kentucky Whigs as they were confidently building campaign machinery for the 1856 presidential election. At a Know-Nothing convention in Philadelphia, Southern delegates insisted on a resolution backing the Kansas-Nebraska Act. Northern delegates promptly walked out and joined the Republican party. Then, the Southern Know-Nothings nominated former President Millard Fillmore for the presidency.

Harlan was tireless in supporting the Whig-American candidates in 1856. A three-hour speech in one town would often soon be followed by a two-hour speech in another. The *Frankfort Commonwealth* reported that each speech of "the young giant of the American party" proclaimed the belief that "Americans should rule America, and that in all cases he would vote for the son of the soil in preference to a foreigner."

It was clear all along, however, that Harlan was fighting for a lost cause. In Kentucky people had begun to worry that a division of the proslavery vote between Fillmore and Democrat James Buchanan might give Republican John C. Frémont the victory. Buchanan won the presidency, and the Fillmore forces lost Kentucky by 6,000 votes. The Democratic victory, plus the fact that Know-Nothing antiforeigner parrotings appeared silly, put an end to the Whig-American combination in Kentucky.

In December, 1856, John Harlan forgot about politics for a while. He married Malvina F. Shanklin of Evansville, Indiana. Mallie Harlan, whose parents were New England abolitionists, came to live in the home of James Harlan, who had a dozen house servants that he and his wife had inherited from their parents. Surprised by the relationship between the elder Harlans and their slaves, Mallie wrote: "The close sympathy existing between the slaves and their Master or Mistress was a source of great wonder to me as a descendant of the Puritans, and I was often obliged to admit to myself that my former views of the 'awful institution of Slavery' would have to be somewhat modified."

Mallie Harlan saw little of the harsh side of slavery—gangs of slaves cultivating and picking cotton from dawn to dark, or children being sold away from their mothers. James Harlan himself freed several of his slaves and helped them make successful starts as free men. One Sunday when James and John Harlan were walking from church, they saw an overseer whipping a group of chained slaves being marched through town. James Harlan stalked angrily up to the man, shook a finger in his face, and said: "You are a damned scoundrel! Good morning, sir!"

On two occasions, James Harlan started suits in the courts in behalf of free Negroes who had been kidnapped and sold into slavery a second time. Denounced as an "abolitionist agent," Harlan wrote a friend that "he who applies that term to me lies in his throat. . . . I have the same opinion of an abolitionist that I have of a disunionist—each deserves the gallows." Like his father, John Harlan ignored all criticism and defended free Negroes in court.

The Harlans' sense of decency made them favor the gradual emancipation of the slaves. But they also contended that government action to end slavery would violate the property rights of American citizens. In the face of increased antislavery agitation by Northern abolitionists and Southern foes like Cassius Clay, the Harlans hardened their attitude. They insisted that slavery was a problem that each state should deal with as it saw fit, and that the national government had the duty to protect the property of slave owners.

In 1858 John Harlan rallied the remnants of the Whigs and was elected judge of the Franklin County court. Then to the surprise of everyone, including Harlan, the twenty-five-year-old county judge was nominated for the United States House of Representatives from the Ashland district that Henry Clay had represented. Democratic newspapers dismissed Harlan by saying that he got the nomination because Whig leaders had no hopes of winning. Soon, however, Harlan's campaign even won the respect of his opponents. The *Frankfort Tri-Weekly Yeoman* grudgingly admitted that he was "clever personally and in point of talent respectable." Whigs gleefully compared Harlan to the young Henry Clay.

The newly reorganized Whigs, now calling themselves the Opposition party, tried to outdo the Democrats in defending slavery. They also quietly junked the anti-foreign slogans of the Whig-Americans and talked instead of the dishonest Democratic officeholders.

It was, however, the slavery issue that took the center of the stage in Harlan's campaign for Congress. This issue became even hotter after the *Dred Scott* decision of the Supreme Court. Dred Scott, a Missouri slave, had sued for his freedom on the ground that residence with his master in the free territory of Wisconsin had made him a free man. Speaking for the Court majority, Chief

Justice Roger Brooke Taney declared that no Negro, free or slave, could be a citizen of the United States. Therefore, Scott had no right to sue for his freedom in federal court. Furthermore, said Taney, even if Scott could sue, his having lived in Wisconsin Territory would not have made him a free man. This was so because the Missouri Compromise of 1820, which forbade slavery in Wisconsin, was unconstitutional. Congress, declared Taney, had no power under the Constitution to prohibit slavery in any territory.

Chief Justice Taney and President Buchanan both innocently thought this decision would settle the slavery question for all time. But they sadly underestimated the depth and bitterness of the antislavery feeling in the nation. Southern Democrats insisted, however, that the *Dred Scott* decision had opened all U.S. territories to slavery and that the federal government had to protect it. Senator Douglas and the Northern Democrats protested that the principle of popular sovereignty had to be followed. The settlers of a territory must be allowed to vote slavery in or out.

Harlan wholeheartedly supported the *Dred Scott* decision. He charged that his Democratic opponent favored Douglas and popular sovereignty. Harlan condemned the idea that a majority of the settlers in a territory could, under popular sovereignty, vote to destroy the property rights of slave owners.

Harlan lost the election by only fifty votes, but more disheartening to him were events in Charleston, South Carolina. The Democratic convention, which met there in the spring of 1860, split over the question of slavery in the territories. Later the Northern wing of the party nominated Senator Douglas. The Southern Democrats nominated John C. Breckinridge of Kentucky, vice-president in the administration of President Buchanan. This split in the Democratic party practically assured the election of Republican Abraham Lincoln. Observing the ruins of the Democratic party, Alexander Stephens of Georgia (soon to become vice-president of the Confederacy) said grimly: "Men will be cutting one another's throats in a little while. In less than 12 months, we shall be in a war, and that the bloodiest in history." A strong Union man, Harlan heard with horror Southern threats that the election of "that Black Republican Lincoln" would bring secession.

Now a man without a party, Harlan worked mightily for the new Constitutional Unionists. This party had nominated the former Whig congressman, John Bell of Tennessee, as its candidate for the presidency. Its platform supported "the Constitution of country, the Union of the states and the enforcement of the laws." The failure even to mention the slavery question caused foes to dub the Unionists the Do-Nothing party.

While Harlan campaigned for Bell, Cassius Clay spoke

throughout the Midwest for Lincoln. Clay looked to the future. Harlan and the Constitutional Unionists looked to the past. They seemed to feel that if they ignored the slavery problem it would somehow go away.

4
★
Harlan Takes His Stand

The election of Lincoln quickly brought about the secession of South Carolina. During the next two months, six other cotton states of the Deep South followed South Carolina out of the Union. Harlan still desperately refused to believe that the Union had been destroyed. He took comfort from the fact that Bell had won Kentucky and had polled forty percent of the vote throughout the South. Believing that a majority of the Southern people supported the Union, Harlan wrote to Kentuckian Joseph Holt, a strong Union man who had been postmaster general and secretary of war in Buchanan's cabinet.

Knowing that Holt was friendly with advisers to Lincoln, Harlan urged him to argue for an immediate withdrawal of federal troops from South Carolina. Ending any threat of force, said Harlan, would win the support of the border slave states (Kentucky, Missouri, Maryland, and Delaware). It would also encourage Unionists in the seceded states to work actively for the return of these states to the Union. Then, Harlan wrote confidently, "the eyes of the country would be directed alone to a National Convention as the only possible mode to settle the present troubles." At this moment Harlan allowed his fear of war to weaken his feeling for the Union. He went on to tell Holt that if it became clear that the people of the seceding states were opposed to the federal government, "they should be allowed to go in peace." The tough, sour-faced Holt, a no-nonsense Union man, filed Harlan's letter and forgot it.

Within a month Fort Sumter was occupied by Confederate forces, and Harlan put all doubts aside. Now that war had come he knew that he had to stand for the Union. Kentucky's Governor Beriah Magoffin had defiantly answered Lincoln's call for 75,000 volunteers. "Your dispatch is received," Magoffin wired back. "In answer, I say emphatically [that] Kentucky will furnish no troops for the wicked purpose of subduing her sister Southern States."

Magoffin was pro-Confederate, while a majority of the Kentucky legislature was pro-Union. Though the people of the state were sharply divided, they did agree on two things. They did not want their slaves confiscated, and they did not want their state to become a battlefield.

Seeing that the legislature would not support him, the governor finally issued a neutrality proclamation on May 20, 1861. It warned the forces of "all other states . . . especially the United and Confederate States" not to enter Kentucky unless invited by the state. Meanwhile Senator John C. Breckinridge had returned home to rally Kentucky to the Confederacy and to "warn Lincoln against his unholy war."

Encouraged by the governor's neutrality proclamation, Breckinridge made plans for a state convention that would either make Magoffin's proclamation permanent or swing Kentucky over to the Confederacy. James and John Marshall Harlan joined Robert J. Breckinridge, an uncle of Senator Breckinridge, in rallying supporters of the Union. Two of Robert Breckinridge's sons, as well as his nephew, supported the Confederacy, as did James B. Clay, son of Henry Clay. In Washington Cassius Clay told Lincoln of the tangled loyalties in Kentucky, but he confidently predicted that Robert Breckinridge could keep the state in the Union.

When Robert Breckinridge heard of his nephew's plans to call a convention, he organized a mass meeting and denounced secession as "utter madness." With the help of the Harlans and Joshua Speed, a long-time friend of Lincoln, Breckinridge had copies of his speech printed and sent all over Kentucky.

John Harlan now plunged into the campaign to elect

pro-Union men to Congress. Copying the rough-and-ready tactics of Cassius Clay, Harlan hired musicians to draw crowds and spoke from a box on Louisville street corners. When election day came, Union men won in nine out of ten congressional districts.

While he spoke publicly for the Union, Harlan was also secretly involved in getting arms and ammunition to Unionists in Kentucky. Both the Unionists and the Confederates had gotten around Governor Magoffin's neutrality proclamation by establishing camps outside the state to train Kentucky troops. The Union camp was across the Ohio River near Cincinnati. A fourth of the men in some Ohio regiments were Kentuckians. The Confederate camp was near Clarksville, Tennessee.

There was also the Kentucky state guard, commanded by General Simon Bolivar Buckner. To keep an eye on the guard, which was considered pro-Confederate, Union men formed a militia outfit called the Home Guard. It was stationed at Camp Dick Robinson near Lexington, and was commanded by William "Bull" Nelson.

Brigadier General Robert Anderson, who had been forced to surrender Fort Sumter, was stationed in Cincinnati as commander of the Kentucky area. He was ordered by Lincoln to get arms both to Nelson's men and to other Unionists. Early one morning Harlan and another man, both heavily armed, met a shipment of guns at a wharf in Louisville and sent it on to Lexington. Soon

"Lincoln rifles" were in the hands of Union men all over Kentucky.

A frustrated Governor Magoffin angrily protested against the activities of both Union and Confederate forces in letters to Lincoln and to President Jefferson Davis of the Confederacy. Lincoln innocently replied that the home guards were Kentuckians who were harming no one. Davis said that the troops at Clarksville were only there to guard Tennessee against invasion. The governor of Tennessee, Isham Harris, backed up Davis' story.

Lincoln's easy-does-it policy toward Kentucky was nearly wrecked by General John C. Frémont, the Union commander in Missouri. In August, 1861, Frémont issued a proclamation that placed the state under military rule and declared that the slaves of all Confederate sympathizers would be confiscated. This news outraged Kentuckians, and one company of volunteers threw down their rifles and went home. Frémont refused to withdraw his proclamation, so Lincoln got rid of Frémont and the proclamation on November 2. When Frémont's supporters complained, the president said he had to act to keep Kentucky in the Union or at least neutral. "I think to lose Kentucky," he wrote, "is nearly the same as to lose the whole game. Kentucky gone, we can not hold Missouri, nor, I think, Maryland. With these all against us . . . the job on our hands is too large for us."

While Kentuckians were still boiling over Frémont's

blunder, the Confederates saved Lincoln further embarrassment by invading Kentucky on September 3, 1861, and planting guns on the Mississippi River at Columbus. Governor Magoffin protested. The Confederates, feeling they had to beat the Union forces to the punch, told Magoffin that the invasion was a "necessity." Then, on September 6, General Ulysses S. Grant sent Union forces into Paducah, another Kentucky town north of Columbus. The Kentucky legislature called on Governor Magoffin to order the state guard to drive the Confederates out of Columbus. It also asked the government in Washington to protect Kentucky from invasion. General Anderson lost no time ordering General George H. Thomas to take command of the troops at Camp Dick Robinson and to recruit more Kentuckians for Union service.

During the days of watchful waiting, John Harlan had stood on a Louisville street and had seen men on one side marching to a Union camp, while men on the other side were heading for a Confederate camp. Then Harlan went to work. He set up headquarters in Lebanon, Kentucky, and traveled into several counties making speeches for the Union and inviting men to join his regiment.

While calling for volunteers, Harlan declared that if the government turned the war into a fight against slavery he would go over to the Confederacy and take his regiment with him. This statement probably helped make his recruiting trips a success. Within two months 1,000 men from strongly proslavery counties had joined Harlan's regiment.

At Camp Robinson the hard, tedious job of drilling troops went on day after day. Each night, the men of the different regiments would gather outside their commanders' quarters and call for a speech. Only one such visit was paid to General Thomas. "Damn this speechmaking!" roared Thomas. "What does a man want to make a speech for?" he asked, and then stomped into his tent.

While some Kentuckians prepared to fight, others began feeling the heavy hand of the federal government. United States marshals were busy charging men with disloyalty to the Union and then throwing them into prison, where they sat for months awaiting trial. Reuben T. Durrett of the *Louisville Courier* was arrested because some of his editorials sounded disloyal. Charles S. Morehead, an ex-governor of Kentucky, was charged with treason and spent four months in military prisons. Lincoln had him released, and Morehead went to England where he made speeches charging that Lincoln had wanted war and had tricked the Confederacy into firing the first shot.

Discussing the people of this notably touchy state, Lincoln quoted a remark by the famous essayist, Ralph Waldo Emerson: "A Kentuckian seems to say by his air and manners, 'Here I am; if you don't like me, the worse for you.'" Proud of their thoroughbred horses, Kentuckians were greatly angered when Union cavalrymen entered the state riding broken down old nags bought in the North from crooked horse traders. Bumbling Secretary of War Simon Cameron's only answer to furious Kentuckians was that he would buy fewer horses.

5

★

Colonel
John Marshall Harlan

In the fall of 1861 John Marshall Harlan, at twenty-eight, was commissioned a colonel commanding the Tenth Kentucky Regiment in the division commanded by General Thomas. Throughout the war, Harlan's regiment fought in no major battles, but it performed its chores efficiently. When General Thomas' command smashed a Confederate invasion of Kentucky at Mill Springs, Harlan's regiment was not in action. It had been sent off to keep an eye on another Confederate force said to be somewhere in the vicinity. Disappointed when he had arrived after the battle of Mill Springs, Harlan let off some steam in a report to headquarters: "All honor to the brave men of Indiana, Kentucky, Minnesota, and Ohio who on that memorable occasion drove back in dismay three times their number of the vandal hordes of secession and trea-son."

Harlan's regiment was then ordered to take a position facing the beaten Southern forces. He reported later that "my men lay on the ground during the whole of Sunday night without fires, tents, overcoats or blankets and with nothing to eat except a fourth of a cracker to each man." The next day Harlan's regiment occupied the Confederate camp and vigorously pursued the rebels.

In the report he made after taking the Confederate camp, Harlan modestly wrote: "I do not claim that any special honor is due my regiment because . . . it first entered the rebel fortifications. . . . Simple justice de-mands the admission that the capture of the enemy's works and property . . . was the result of the battle . . . on the 19th." Again Harlan, as he frequently did, praised the endurance and loyalty of his men. "I do claim for the officers and soldiers of this regiment that, under circum-stances the most discouraging, they made a march which indicated their willingness, even eagerness, to endure any fatigue or make any sacrifice in order to meet on the field of battle those wicked and unnatural men who are seeking without cause to destroy the Union of our fathers."

Even when reporting to his superior officers, the young soldier could not refrain from writing a speech praising his men and denouncing the enemy. If any of Harlan's Know-Nothing opposition to Catholicism still lingered, it swiftly disappeared as he observed the valor and self-sacrifice of the many Catholics in his regiment. Years later he wrote, "It was a magnificent sight to see how the boys struggled through mud and rain to reach the field of battle. . . . I see now with great distinctness old Father Nash pushing along on foot with the boys. . . . Equally earnest with him was a Catholic priest from Washington County, who had come with Catholic soldiers from that county."

Harlan's military fame resulted from Confederate raider John H. Morgan's daring assault on Union supply lines in December, 1862. Morgan had been harassing Union commanders in Kentucky, but he found Harlan tough opposition. Moving with great speed, Harlan's command overtook Morgan, attacked him, and forced the raider to retreat before he could destroy important railroad bridges. Other Union forces then drove Morgan from the state. In his report, Harlan again was modest. "I do not suppose that the engagement which my command had with Morgan's forces could properly be called a battle, the main bodies of the respective forces not being engaged. . . . [But] it is certain that after my command drove the rebel chieftain across the Rolling Fork [River] in such a precipitate manner, he abandoned the railroad, and very soon thereafter fled from the state."

Harlan's superior wrote headquarters, "Colonel Harlan, for energy, promptness, and success in pursuing and driving rebel forces from the railroad, is entitled to the gratitude not only of the people of Kentucky, but of the whole Army of the Cumberland. He is, in my opinion, entitled to special notice from the commanding general."

During 1862 the Radical Republican and abolitionist drive for emancipation of the slaves gained power in Congress. Fearing that such a move would drive the border slave states from the Union, Lincoln countered it with plans for gradual compensated emancipation. But the border slave states refused to go along. They echoed the near-sighted view of old Senator J.H. Crittenden of Kentucky: "Let slavery alone. It will go out like a candle." That is, it would die out on its own.

On July 12, 1862, Congress struck its hardest blow at slavery. It passed the Confiscation Act, which declared "forever free" the slaves of owners who supported the Confederacy and authorized Lincoln to recruit Negroes for army service. Lincoln reluctantly signed this act but did little to enforce it. Then he again met with congressmen from the border slave states. He warned them that slavery would be destroyed if the war lasted much longer. Therefore it was to their advantage to support gradual emancipation. The border state men balked again. They argued that compensated emancipation would cost too much, and also would merely make the Confederacy more determined to fight to the finish.

After this futile meeting, Lincoln concluded that emancipation had become "a military necessity, absolutely essential for the salvation of the Union." On July 22,

Lincoln read his Emancipation Proclamation to the members of his cabinet. Secretary of State William H. Seward urged Lincoln to delay the proclamation until Union forces had won a victory. The war news had not been good for many weeks. Lincoln agreed to wait a while.

While Lincoln waited for good news from his armies, Cassius Clay returned from Russia, where he had served as American minister. He urged Lincoln to free the slaves quickly. Otherwise, Clay warned, England and other European nations might recognize the Confederacy and give it aid. Still worried about the border states, Lincoln said: "Kentucky would go against us. And we have as much as we can carry."

"You are mistaken," Clay insisted. "The Kentuckians have heard this question discussed by me for a quarter of a century and all have made up their minds. Those who intend to stand by slavery have already joined the rebel army, and those who remain will stand by the Union. Not a man of intelligence will change his mind."

Following the Union victory at Antietam, which blocked the Confederate invasion of Maryland, Lincoln issued the preliminary Emancipation Proclamation on September 22. It declared that all persons held as slaves within any state or part of a state that was in rebellion against the United States would be free on and forever after January 1, 1863.

The proclamation won the support of the British working people, which practically ended the Confederacy's chances of gaining aid from Britain. That nation had freed the slaves in its colonies many years before and hesitated to support a government that favored slavery.

The proclamation also quieted a noisy group of Republican governors who were meeting to complain about Lincoln's conduct of the war. But it pleased few other people. Radical Republicans and abolitionists said the proclamation was a sly attempt by Lincoln to stall enforcement of the Confiscation Act. They said that this act, which freed the slaves of all disloyal owners no matter *where* they lived, went farther than the proclamation to smash slavery. It was true that the proclamation did not free any slaves immediately. Neither did it apply to the slaves in border slave states. There were, however, angry outbursts from these states. The mildest was a comment by the *Louisville Democrat* that "the abolitionists have pressed him [Lincoln] into their service."

The Confederacy bitterly denounced the proclamation as an invitation for the slaves to murder their masters. Northern Democrats who supported the war accused Lincoln of turning the conflict into a fight to take people's property away from them. Some officers resigned from the Union army in protest.

Using the proclamation as a campaign issue, the Democrats made heavy gains in the congressional elections in November. They came close to electing enough congressmen to control Congress. But the border slave states sent enough Union men to Congress to keep the Repub-

licans in control. In these states Lincoln's policy of keeping hands off slavery but laying heavy hands on any person
suspected of being "disloyal" paid off in a Union party
victory at the polls. Critics said Lincoln prayed every
night: "Oh, Lord, we earnestly hope that Thou will favor
our cause, but we *must* have Kentucky." And that tough
Kentucky Unionist, Lincoln's friend Joseph Holt, saw to
it that his state remained loyal to the Union. As judge
advocate general, Holt had the power to throw "disloyal"
persons in jail and keep them there without trial. He felt
that men ought to be persuaded to support the Union, but
if they were stubborn, they should be jailed. Throughout
the nation, an estimated 38,000 "stubborn" men were
imprisoned during the Civil War.

During December, debate raged over the proclamation,
and people wondered if Lincoln would sign it on January
1. Late in December Lincoln was warned by General
Horatio Wright, who commanded troops in Ohio and
Kentucky, that state officials might take Kentucky out of
the Union if the Emancipation Proclamation was signed.
Wright asked permission to keep a force near the capital
of Frankfort which would be prepared to arrest anyone
who favored secession. The next day Wright was told to
take any action he felt was necessary. On January 1 Lincoln signed the proclamation, which he justified as a "fit
and necessary war measure." A committee of the Kentucky House of Representatives denounced it and the
arming of Negroes as acts of tyranny and crimes against

civilization. But no other action was taken by Kentuckians, and Wright's troops weren't needed.

John Marshall Harlan, as would be expected, denounced the Emancipation Proclamation as "unconstitutional and null and void." But, as Cassius Clay had predicted, most Kentucky Unionists remained loyal, and Harlan was among them. A few weeks later, his father died and Harlan went back home to settle family affairs. Feeling that he had to take over his father's law practice to "preserve from loss and waste what he had fairly earned by hard work," Harlan resigned from the army. But his letter to his commanding officer showed no weakening of his attachment to the Union. "If, therefore, I am permitted to retire from the army, I beg the commanding general to feel assured that it is from no want of confidence in the justice or ultimate triumph of the Union cause. That cause will always have the warmest sympathies of my heart, for there are no conditions upon which I will consent to a dissolution of the Union."

Harlan did not keep his promise to lead his regiment into the Confederate army if the goverment attacked slavery. And there is no evidence that his men complained because he failed to do this. In fact the members of Harlan's regiment had great respect for their leader. They bragged during and after the war that their young colonel could outrun, outjump, and outwrestle any of his men. They told how Harlan regularly urged them to be brave, to stand up to the enemy, and not to run. But Harlan had cheerfully admitted after one skirmish that he felt like running but couldn't because he was an officer. Harlan had also won the respect and love of his men by doing things like putting his shoulder to the wheel of a wagon mired in the mud or swinging his ax to cut trees needed to repair roads.

6

★

Kentucky Politics Again

Soon after leaving the army, Harlan went back into politics. The Democrats, under the title of the Union party, were in control of Kentucky. The Whig party to which Harlan had belonged was defunct. He shunned the antislavery Republicans and joined the Union party. At that party's convention in 1863, Harlan received a unanimous nomination for attorney general. Responding to this honor, he called for "our earnest prosecution of the war . . . discarding the idea of peace on any terms other than submission of the rebels to the laws which they have outraged."

Although Harlan was a Union man, he opposed the "dangerous policies" of President Lincoln. In his successful campaign for attorney general, Harlan attacked the Emancipation Proclamation and Lincoln's policy of permitting Union officers to imprison suspected Confederate sympathizers without a hearing before a judge. Even Robert Breckinridge, who had led the fight to keep Kentucky in the Union, angrily protested to Lincoln against military rule in Kentucky.

Kentucky's opposition to the enrollment of Negroes for army service soon threatened to bring a clash between state troops and Union forces. The newly elected governor, Thomas E. Bramlette, declared on September 1, 1863, that making a soldier out of a Negro "humiliates the just pride of loyal men." He then announced that "if the President does not, upon my demand, stop the Negro enrollment, I will."

Lieutenant Governor Richard Jacob wrote Lincoln, begging him to delay the enrollment, as there was serious danger of "producing an outbreak of a portion of our loyal people, and I dreadfully fear a conflict between the Federal and State authorities."

Robert Breckinridge then conferred with Governor Bramlette, Harlan, and other officials. He strongly urged that no step be taken which might lead to bloodshed. Bramlette cooled off and issued a proclamation urging people not to resist the Negro enrollment. He promised that the arming of Negroes would be delayed. Lincoln later agreed not to enroll Negroes in any part of Kentucky that furnished its full quota of white men for the Union army.

During 1864 Harlan was personally involved with the

buying and selling of slaves for the first and only time in his life. Lincoln's Emancipation Proclamation did not, of course, apply to Kentucky, a border slave state. When his father's estate was settled, Harlan's mother was entitled to only one-third of the property, which included a dozen slaves. Harlan was worried because this division of the estate would leave his mother with only four servants. He also had a real affection for the slaves who had served his parents for so many years. Therefore, he made himself financially responsible to the estate for all of the slaves and left them with his mother. Aside from wanting to provide for his mother's comfort, Harlan could not bear, according to Mallie, "to think of these slaves falling into other hands through the barter and sale of human beings that was still in vogue."

At this time John and Mallie set up housekeeping in their own home. The Harlans bought a Negro cook from a young couple who were leaving Kentucky. When the cook and Mallie could not agree on how the kitchen should be run, the Harlans gave the cook her freedom. Then they bought another woman who had begged them to take her so that she would not be sold out of the state and separated from her husband.

Although he personally wanted little to do with slavery, Harlan still stubbornly defended the rights of slave owners. His opposition to emancipation, the arming of Negroes, and the wholesale arrest of persons accused of "disloyalty" led Harlan to support General George B. Mc-Clellan, the Democratic presidential candidate in 1864. Harlan campaigned for McClellan throughout Kentucky and he also spoke in Indiana against Governor Oliver P. Morton, a Lincoln supporter who was seeking reelection. During a speech in New Albany, Indiana, Harlan said: "The triumph of abolition would be the triumph of a spirit, which, in order to effect its purpose, would not hesitate to trample upon the Constitution and the law."

Harlan's trip to Indiana brought a sharp attack on him by the *Frankfort Commonwealth*. "Is it not inconsistent and ungrateful for any citizen of Kentucky professing Unionism . . . to take an active part in the attempt to defeat Governor Morton? . . . Col. Harlan, once an unconditional Union man, has cast his lot with those who were from the first with the rebellion."

Harlan protested that he was fighting not Unionism but emancipation of the slaves and other attacks on a citizen's rights by Lincoln and his followers. Harlan still clung to the Whig view that slavery was each state's own "business" to handle as it saw fit. Lincoln had finally abandoned this Whig doctrine when he issued the Emancipation Proclamation though he had argued that emancipation was a "military necessity" to save the Union. But Harlan and other border state men stubbornly believed they could defend the Union *and* slavery. They were slow to recognize the hard fact that the war for the

Union had become a war for the freedom of a race in bondage. Events had left Harlan behind, and it would be several years before he caught up with the times.

In the November election, McClellan won only three states—Kentucky, Delaware, and New Jersey—and Lincoln was reelected easily. In his annual message to Congress on December 6, 1864, the president reminded the members of some unfinished business. During the previous session, a proposed amendment abolishing slavery had passed the Senate but had failed to gain the two-thirds majority vote required in the House. Lincoln said the election results clearly showed that the new Congress, which would meet in March, 1865, was sure to pass the amendment. But he did not want to wait. He challenged the House to take the final step that would kill slavery forever.

Lincoln then went to work, using all his powers of persuasion to get certain Democratic congressmen to change their minds and support the amendment. He got strong support from Representative James S. Rollins of Missouri, one of the largest slaveholders in that border slave state. During debate on the Thirteenth Amendment, Rollins interrupted the proceedings to say he had received word that Missouri had abolished slavery by state action. Then he said, "I am no longer the owner of a slave, and I thank God for it. . . . I say with all my heart, let them go." He went on to mourn the "wickedness and folly" of Kentucky men who led the opposition to Lincoln's plan for gradual emancipation. "If ever a people made a mistake," said Rollins, "it was the men of Kentucky."

On January 31, 1865, the Thirteenth Amendment was passed by the House with three votes to spare. Ten Democrats, prodded and cajoled by Lincoln, had joined the Republicans to pass the measure.

Harlan was not ready to admit that the men of Kentucky had made a mistake. In an angry speech at Lexington, he said, "If there were not a dozen slaves in the state of Kentucky, I should oppose the amendment." He insisted that it was "a flagrant invasion" of states' rights and "a violation of promises made to Kentucky slaveholders." In another speech later that year, Harlan lashed out at the Thirteenth Amendment as an example of the "tyranny of the majority," which "confers upon a bare majority of Congress the power" to take property away from slaveholders.

Kentucky's strong support for Democrat McClellan in the 1864 election had done little to smooth relations between that state and the federal government. An investigator for Secretary of War Edwin M. Stanton reported that Governor Bramlette's policy was "simply self first, state second, Union last." The trouble with Kentuckians, said one of Stanton's men, was that the government had treated them so gently that they had "become more violent in their denunciations of the administration than the original rebels. A large majority of Kentuckians are today undoubtedly disloyal."

Suiting his actions to these words, General Stephen G. Burbridge, the Union commander in Kentucky, suddenly declared the state to be under military law. He also ordered Governor Bramlette to disband all state forces and send the men home. Burbridge charged that these troops were working secretly with Confederate raiders.

Protests from irate Bramlette supporters poured into Washington, and Lincoln quickly set aside the Burbridge order. He also studied a statement by General Grant, who had been Union commander in the West. Grant said the fumble-fisted Burbridge lacked the good sense and patience to win the cooperation of Kentuckians. Deciding that the state would never simmer down while Burbridge was in command, Lincoln removed him. The *Louisville Journal* joyfully announced on February 10, 1865: "Maj. Gen. John M. Palmer of Ill. has been appointed to command in Kentucky. Thank God and Pres. Lincoln."

Most Kentuckians were ready to forgive and forget past wrongs, and Palmer was warmly greeted by members of the Kentucky legislature at a special meeting. But this era of good feeling did not last long. Palmer continued Burbridge's policy of arming Negroes. In fact, he speeded it up after Congress passed an act freeing the wives and children of all Negroes who enlisted to fight for the Union.

Palmer's program of military emancipation brought an immediate attack from Harlan. He condemned the aid given "large bodies of Negro men, women and children in the state, at the expense of the nation, and with a watchful care which has never been exhibited for the wives and families of the white soldiers of Kentucky." He went on to denounce the policy whereby Kentucky's "large slave population is suddenly dumped in our midst," and to warn that emancipation "will destroy the peace and security of the white man in Kentucky."

The surrender of General Lee's Army of Northern Virginia at Appomattox Courthouse and the tragic death of Lincoln then plunged the nation into problems of peace that were to prove as difficult as those of war.

7

★

War in Congress

On the day that he was mortally wounded by the half-mad John Wilkes Booth, Lincoln told his cabinet that he hoped to bring all the Southern states back into the Union before Congress met again in December. He was rightfully worried about what Congress might do when it went to work. The Radical Republicans, led by the shrewd Representative Thaddeus Stevens of Pennsylvania and the stubborn Senator Charles Sumner of Massachusetts, strongly opposed Lincoln's "forgive and forget" policy toward the South. Lincoln proposed to let each Southern state establish a government when ten percent of its citizens took an oath of allegiance to the United States. Radicals protested that this speedy organization of state governments in the South would turn the ex-slaves over to "the incurable slaveholders." Stevens said the South must be "reduced to hopeless feebleness." Sumner argued that the Southern states had "committed suicide" when they seceded and that they should not be allowed back in the Union until they granted Negroes equal rights and the vote.

When Lincoln died the Radicals felt that their plans for the South would have smooth sailing. His successor, Andrew Johnson of Tennessee, was the only Southern senator who had remained loyal to the Union, and he had frequently denounced Confederate officials as "traitors." But Johnson soon gave the Radicals some surprises. He approved the state governments Lincoln had organized in Virginia, Tennessee, Louisiana, and Arkansas. Then he began appointing provisional governors in other Southern states. State conventions were held to write new constitutions, and then elections for new governments were held— elections in which no Negroes were allowed to vote. By the fall of 1865, governments were at work in all the ex-Confederate states except Texas.

The angry Radicals grumbled that Johnson had put back into power in the South many of the men who had fought for the Confederacy and who were opposed to granting the Negro equal rights. One Radical said this amounted to leaving "the fate of the lamb to the hyena."

The new state governments now played into the hands of Stevens and his Radicals by enacting "Black Codes" to control the Negro and to keep him subservient. These codes were harsher in some states than in others, but all of them gave the white man about as much control over the Negro as slave owners had had before the war. Georgia, for example, declared that "all persons strolling about in idleness" would be put in chain gangs and hired out to white men. Throughout the North, many people angrily denounced the Black Codes as a brazen attempt by the South to reestablish slavery under another name.

The ex-vice-president of the Confederacy, Alexander Stephens, and Generals Robert E. Lee and Wade Hampton, among others, deplored the passage of the Black Codes and the Southern states' refusal to let any Negroes vote. In vain, they urged the states to give the vote to educated, property-owning Negroes. But the South shunned the educated black, as it shunned the illiterate field hand. Unfortunately for the future peace of the South and the nation, Southerners had been treating blacks as property, as "things," for so long that they could not think of them as free men. During the entire time the Southern states were allowed to operate under Johnson's mild reconstruction plan, nothing was done to educate the Negro or to give him the vote. Instead, Negro schools were burned and teachers from the North were harassed and run out of town.

The final insult, as far as the Radical Republicans were concerned, came when Congress assembled on December 4, 1865. Among the representatives and senators from the South were no less than seventy-four former Confederate army officers and government officials. All of these men had been given special pardons by President Johnson so that they could serve in Congress. Radical Republicans stormed at the presence of the ex-Confederates who had been trying to destroy the government a few months before.

Bowing to the wishes of Thaddeus Stevens, Congress refused to let the ex-Confederates take their seats in the Senate and House. Then Congress established the Joint Committee on Reconstruction to study conditions in the South. It was composed of six senators and nine representatives and generally was called the Committee of Fifteen. Ably bossed by Stevens, this committee let it be known that Congress, not the president, was going to take control of reconstruction in the South.

Seeking a test of strength with Johnson, Stevens introduced a bill to extend the life of the Freedmen's Bureau, which had been authorized by Congress to operate for only one year. The bureau had done useful work in the South, giving guidance to Negroes and food to both blacks and whites. Its foes accused the bureau of "spoiling" the Negro with education and spending too much time drumming up votes for the Republican party.

Johnson vetoed the Freedmen's Bureau bill, and the Radicals failed to muster the necessary two-thirds majority needed to override his veto. Then Johnson made an unwise speech denouncing the Radicals. Congress, which had let Lincoln have his way when the nation was in danger, was in no mood to listen to a presidential lecture. In April of 1866 Stevens rammed through Congress a civil rights bill to protect Negroes from the Black Codes. Johnson vetoed the bill, but Congress, still angered by his earlier speech, overrode the veto.

The Civil Rights Act of 1866 provided that all persons born in the United States were citizens and should have the right to make contracts, sue and be sued, give evidence in court, buy and sell property, and in general have equal rights under the law no matter what their race or color. Later, in July of 1866, Congress passed another Freedmen's Bureau bill and overrode the president's veto.

Taking no chances that Congress might later change or repeal the Civil Rights Act of 1866, Stevens and Sumner secured passage of the Fourteenth Amendment. No constitutional amendment in the nation's history is more important than the fourteenth. The first section of this amendment declares that anyone born or naturalized in the United States is a citizen and that "no state shall make or enforce any law which shall abridge the privileges or immunities of citizens of the United States; nor shall any state deprive any person of life, liberty, or property without due process of law; nor deny to any person . . . the equal protection of the laws."

The Southern states were informed by Congress that they could not get back into the Union until they ratified the Fourteenth Amendment. Since their senators and representatives were still waiting to take their seats in Congress, the Southern states were in no mood to take orders. All Southern states except Tennessee rejected the amendment. It was rumored that President Johnson advised these states to refuse to ratify it. If he had, he made a big mistake—one that the shrewd Stevens and his Radicals were quick to seize upon.

8
★
Man in the Middle

When the war ended John Marshall Harlan again was a man in search of a party. In the summer of 1865, those Kentuckians who had supported the Confederacy held a higher place in the state than those who had supported the Union. The Democratic party, which was all-powerful in the South, was controlled by ex-Confederates. It might be said that Kentucky "seceded" from the Union *after* the Civil War ended. Richard Jacob, a Union man and lieutenant governor of Kentucky during the war, said: "Every man within the realm of the state knows that no man who has been for the Union has the slightest chance for position. The test is not honesty, not capability, not democracy, but were you 'for the Union or for the Lost Cause.'"

After the Whig party died Harlan supported the Constitutional Union party. During the war, Harlan and other ex-Whigs worked with Democrats in the Union party. Shunned now by the pro-Confederates, and wanting nothing to do with the pro-Negro Radical Republicans, Harlan again sought a middle ground, as he had in 1860. He joined the Conservative Union party. The first meeting of the party took place in 1866 just two months after Secretary of State Seward had announced on December 18, 1865, that the Thirteenth Amendment abolishing slavery had been ratified by the necessary three-fourths of the states. The Conservative Unionists realized that it would be futile to oppose emancipation. So they accepted the Thirteenth Amendment and concentrated their attacks on the Radical Republican program in Congress. Though he owned few slaves, Harlan was defiant to the end. He publicly announced that he had not freed his slaves until forced by law to do so.

In attacking Radical Republican measures to aid the Negroes, the Conservative Unionists used President Johnson as a symbol. They praised Johnson "for the bold and patriotic stand he has taken against the Radicals in the Congress . . . especially shown by his recent veto message of the Freedmen's Bill."

Harlan did not run for office in 1866, but he kept busy making campaign speeches. Opposing the Civil Rights Act of 1866 and the Fourteenth Amendment, he charged that the Radicals were aiming to deny the vote "to almost the entire white population" of the South while giving the vote to the Negro. "The permanent triumph," he warned, "of those who in the North are following the lead of Sumner and Stevens in their series of Constitutional amendments would work a complete revolution in our . . . system of government, and most probably the overthrow of constitutional liberty." At the same time, Harlan condemned the leaders of the Democratic party as "the disunionists of 1861." He emphasized that the Conservative Union party "denounced the heresies of secession and rebellion while . . . they denounced the fanaticism of the North."

Harlan's attempt to pronounce "a plague on both your houses" met with no success. The *Cincinnati Weekly Gazette* chided him, "There are but two parties in Kentucky. You must go to the one or to the other. . . . If you choose to attempt a middle party, well and good. In some places, the rebels will beat you; in others, the Radicals."

The split of the vote between the Conservative Unionists and the Republicans gave the Democrats in Kentucky a clean sweep in the 1866 elections and left the Conservative Union organization in a shambles. The *Gazette* summed it all up neatly: "[The members of] the Conservative party have lived their day. . . . They have failed, miserably failed, and henceforth must get out of the way. There is no room . . . for [this party]. The issues before the people won't admit of being split into three sets of principles, and these Union Conservatives henceforth must go over and join the rebel camp or come out like men and fight for positive, tangible Union principles."

On the national political battlefront Harlan also saw Johnson, his symbol of opposition to Radical Republicanism, soundly defeated in the congressional elections of November, 1866. The Northern voters cast their ballots for a stern policy toward the South that had passed anti-Negro Black Codes and had rejected the Fourteenth Amendment. Radical Republicans won a big enough majority in the Senate and House to easily override any veto by President Johnson.

The new Congress, which opened in March of 1867, quickly passed a Reconstruction Act which swept aside the state governments that had been operating in the South for more than a year. It divided the South into five military districts, each ruled by a general. These military governors set up an election system that permitted Negroes as well as whites to vote for convention delegates who then wrote new state constitutions. These new constitutions were far more liberal than those they replaced. For the first time the common people had a voice in running local and state governments in the South. (Before the war, for example, less than 200 men had controlled South Carolina.)

Many Negroes were elected to state legislatures during the Reconstruction years. But Negroes controlled no Southern state, and in none of the legislatures did they have a majority. The new Reconstruction governments, established by Negroes and white Radical Republicans, did do much to improve living conditions in the South. They repealed the Black Codes, lifted the tax burden from small farmers, and set up the first system of public education in the South. Money was spent on state services for the benefit of the people that prewar governments had ignored. This attempt to catch up with the rest of the country—particularly in the field of public education—cost a lot of money. There was waste and corruption. But weighed against the good done, the amount of graft and stealing was not high. Certainly, the graft was not as rampant as in New York City where the Democrats' Boss Tweed stole millions, or in Washington where members of Congress and cabinet officials frequently took bribes and winked at corruption.

Watching events in Congress during 1867, Harlan had occasion to recall his warning against the "tyranny of the majority." The Radical Republican majority, which had rammed the Reconstruction program through Congress over President Johnson's veto, was not through harassing him. On the same day in March that the first Reconstruction bill became law, Congress passed the Tenure of Office Act. It forbade the president to remove from office civil officials, even including the members of his own cabinet, without the consent of the Senate.

When Johnson challenged Congress by attempting to remove Secretary of War Stanton from office, wild charges were made that the president was trying to become a dictator. On February 24, 1868, the House impeached the president "for high crimes and misdemeanors," and the Senate prepared to sit as a court to try him. At that point, Senator William Pitt Fessenden of Maine jolted fellow Republicans by opposing the impeachment. He said Johnson was not guilty of any crime other than opposing the program of the Radical Republicans. He felt the conviction of Johnson on such flimsy charges would destroy the power of the presidency. Thereafter, said Fessenden, any president who opposed a majority of the members of Congress faced the threat of impeachment. Led by Fessenden, six more Republicans voted for acquittal, and the Radicals failed by one vote to get the two-thirds majority needed to convict Johnson. These Republicans had courageously placed their respect for the office of the presidency above their opposition to Johnson.

9

★

Break with the Past

The Negroes' newly won right to vote stirred up opposition and violence in Kentucky, as it did in other Southern states. The Ku Klux Klan, which had been organized in Tennessee in December of 1865, soon spread throughout the South. The Klan was not as strong in Kentucky as elsewhere, but it was active. Its hooded riders broke up political meetings and whipped and killed blacks. White men who dared support the Negro drive for equal rights were also beaten and killed. In Kentucky the counties of Marion, Madison, Mercer, Boyle, and Lincoln were terrorized by Klansmen and other raiders called "The Regulators," "Rowzee's Band," and "Skagg's Men."

While Kentucky politics flickered and flamed with violence, Cassius Clay came home to Madison County from his post in Russia. Remembering Clay's long fight against slavery, plantation owners blamed him for the loss of their slaves. Clay defied his neighbors by arming Negroes and marching them to the polls on election day. Night riders struck back at him, burning his barns, stealing his horses and cattle, and scaring off his servants. Later, in 1872, the unpredictable Clay turned against President Grant and supported Horace Greeley, the presidential candidate of both the Liberal Republicans and the Democrats. Then Clay's Radical Republican friends deserted him, but the "Old Lion of White Hall" refused to be driven from his home.

The collapse of the Conservative Unionists in 1867 had again left Harlan a man without a party. He retired from politics and went into a law partnership in Louisville with Benjamin H. Bristow, a Lincoln supporter and Union soldier during the Civil War. Harlan kept busy with his law practice, but he could not ignore the reports of widespread lynchings and whippings of Negroes, which the state government chose to ignore. Harlan felt that he had to get back into politics to speak out for law and decency. He could not join the Democratic party which had opposed the Union during the war and now condoned the terror. Should he join the Republicans? They had strongly backed the Thirteenth and Fourteenth Amendments, which Harlan long had opposed. Now, however, he had begun to feel that these amendments were necessary to protect Negro rights and rebuild the union of states. A man with a strong sense of justice, Harlan also concluded that the changing times made it necessary for a man of honesty to change his mind.

While Harlan debated his future political course, he was deeply stirred by a clash between pro-Southern and pro-Union factions in the Kentucky Presbyterian Church. The pro-Southern faction, headed by leaders of the Democratic party, broke away from the national church, which had supported the Union cause during the war. As he had in 1861, Harlan threw his support to Robert J. Breckinridge, leader of the pro-Union faction. As the Unionists' lawyer, Harlan fought several court battles when pro-Southerners tried to seize church property owned by pro-Union congregations. This bitter religious fight gave Harlan another strong reason for not joining the Democratic party. His decision to join the Republicans may have been influenced by his wife or by his law partner, Bristow, who later became secretary of the treasury in Grant's cabinet. At any rate, Harlan and several other Conservative Unionists campaigned for Grant in 1868.

In 1871, only three years after he had joined the Republicans, Harlan was nominated unanimously for the governorship. All the fire he had previously displayed in attacking Republicanism was now summoned in its defense. And Governor Morton of Indiana, who had been opposed by Harlan in 1864, made a speech for the Kentuckian.

Harlan agreed to a series of debates with the Democratic candidate, Preston B. Leslie, though he knew this would give his opponent a perfect chance to make him eat his anti-Republican words in public. In the first debate, Leslie immediately lashed at Harlan as a "weathercock" who turned whichever way the political wind blew. He reminded voters that Harlan had said a few years earlier that Republican policy "was revolutionary, and if carried out would result in the destruction of our free government." That, said Leslie, "was a correct view of it."

Harlan defended Republican policies and said it was futile for Kentuckians to oppose the Thirteenth, Fourteenth, and Fifteenth Amendments, which freed the Negro, gave him citizenship, and granted him the vote. He said these amendments were necessary "to place it beyond the power of any state to interfere with the results of the war." He said the Democratic policy of opposition to Negro rights was "suicidal and ruinous," and begged the people not to "enter upon a career of agitation which can bring the state no good . . . and can only tend to isolate us from the balance of our countrymen."

When his Democratic opponent read quotations from Harlan's earlier anti-Negro speeches, Harlan coolly replied: "Let it be said that I am right rather than consistent." In another speech replying to charges of not being consistent, Harlan said: "It can be said of *no* man that he has changed *no* opinions within the last ten years." Never trying to ignore his antislavery past, Harlan told another audience: "It is true, fellow citizens, that almost the entire people of Kentucky, at one period in their history, were opposed to freedom, citizenship and suffrage of the Colored race. It is true that I was at one time in my life opposed to conferring these privileges upon them, but I have lived long enough to feel and declare, as I do this night, that the most perfect despotism that ever existed on this earth was the institution of African slavery. It was an enemy to free speech; it was an enemy to good government; it was an enemy to a free press.

"The time was, and not long ago in Kentucky, when any declaration such as I now make against the institution of slavery would have imperiled my life in many portions of the state. With slavery it was death or tribute. It knew no compromise, it tolerated no middle course. I rejoice that it is gone."

At this time Congress sought to quell the terrorist attacks by masked riders through the Ku Klux Klan Act. Harlan vigorously defended this act against the criticism of Leslie and other Democratic speakers. "For myself," said Harlan, "I have no terms to make with that band of murderers and assassins denominated Ku Klux, nor shall I have any terms to make with them if I shall have the honor to become Chief Magistrate of this Commonwealth."

Harlan ignored the taunts of hostile crowds to support the Civil Rights Act of 1866. "Thousands of gallant men in the State of Kentucky," he declared, "owe their lives to that bill and to the fact that it opened the doors of the Federal courts for the protection of their lives, their liberty and their property. Had the Federal Government, after conferring freedom on the slaves, left them to the tender mercies of those who were unwilling to protect them in life, liberty and property, it would have deserved the contempt of free men the world over." Harlan then went on to condemn the refusal to let a Negro testify against a white man in a state court as being "directly promotive of outrage."

Early in the campaign Harlan clearly saw that new issues were needed to turn the voters' attention away from the bitterness of the war and Reconstruction. He found one issue in the vast agricultural, mineral, and manufacturing resources of his state. Pointing out that Ohio and Illinois were easily outstripping Kentucky in population and business growth, Harlan charged that Democratic policy had driven Kentuckians to other states. In this connection, he contended that Kentucky's transportation system and, as a result, its business growth had been hindered for years by the virtual monopoly enjoyed by the Louisville and Nashville Railroad. Men in Cincinnati and Lexington had proposed to build a rival railroad, but their plea for a franchise had been denied by the Kentucky legislature. Harlan accused the Democrats of opposing the Cincinnati Southern Railway solely because of a senseless dislike of a Northern city.

Swinging from his attack on the railroad monopoly, Harlan next charged that the Democrats planned to substitute "direct taxation" of property for the indirect income tax favored by the Republicans. The former, he argued, would tax "farms, houses, land, implements and tools" at the same rate as it taxed "the incomes . . . of the wealthy," and would place unjust burdens on the poor. Harlan contended that the national government "foresaw that the poor man would have to fight the battles of the country and hence determined to make the rich man pay the taxes." Years later, as an associate justice of the Supreme Court, Harlan delivered a powerful opinion supporting the graduated income tax based on ability to pay.

During his campaign, Harlan rode horseback through eastern Kentucky, talking to the sturdy mountaineers who had served in his regiment. According to Mallie, her husband saw a great future for these self-reliant mountaineers because of the opportunity for education that finally was being given to them. This interest in the welfare of the common people caused Harlan to bitterly attack the state's "rate-bill" system of financing education. It provided that if more money were needed in a school district, it should be obtained by assessments upon local families in proportion to the number of children they had in school. Harlan angrily said that this provision meant "that the poor man blessed in the number of his children, but unprovided with the world's goods, is taxed, while the rich who are able to educate their children in private schools are exempt from taxation." Declaring that "when war menaced the country, it was the poor and the sons of the poor who sprang to its defense," Harlan insisted "the rich owed it to the poor to contribute to the education of the latter." Harlan's respect and compassion for the common man, which had been strengthened during the war, influenced his actions when he went on to the Supreme Court.

The Republican candidate's steady hammering away at the issues of economic progress and equalizing the tax burdens won him increasing support in the state. It became clear that Harlan was going to roll up a record vote for his party. His opponent, Leslie, sought to shift the voters' attention to the dangers he claimed the state faced if the Republicans won. Leslie pointed out that Kentucky's debt in 1867 was $7,000,000, and four years later, under Democratic rule, it was only $1,000,000. But in Louisiana, the state debt had skyrocketed from $7,000,000 to $40,-000,000 during four years of Radical Republican rule. Leslie let these figures sink in. Then he told voters it was easy to see how short a time it would take the Republicans to "do" the people of Kentucky out of forty or fifty millions. Why, demanded Leslie, should the state "exchange its present honest and economically administered government for such a rule of robbery, ruin, and disgrace as these Radicals have brought upon every other state, where, by fraud or force, or both, they have been 'clothed on' with power."

Kentuckians had been thrilled by Harlan's vision of the state's future growth, but Leslie's scare talk made a more lasting impression on many voters.

The Harlan-Leslie contest was further enlivened when Negroes attacked segregation on the horse-drawn streetcars of Louisville. Their campaign began when a black man named Robert Fox boarded a streetcar and sat down in the section reserved for whites. He refused to move and was thrown off the car by the driver. Fox sued the streetcar company in federal district court. The judge told the jury that under federal law common carriers must treat all passengers alike. The jury then awarded Fox damages of $15.00, plus $72.50 in legal costs. Democratic officials of the city and state criticized the Fox decision. The streetcar company ignored the court's decision and continued to segregate passengers.

A few days later a Negro boy boarded a streetcar and sat in the white section. This time the driver merely stopped the car and refused to move until the boy sat in the other section. While city and state officials looked on, a mob of white teen-agers dragged the Negro boy from the car and began to beat him. When the boy finally started defending himself, the police arrested him for disturbing the peace. The boy was tried in a city court and the magistrate ruled that streetcar companies were not required to treat blacks the same as whites. He fined the boy and warned that further attempts by blacks to desegregate streetcars would bring firm action by the police.

The Louisville Negroes refused to back down. During the next week, dozens of streetcars were boarded by blacks who took seats in the white section. Drivers left the cars, and occasionally Negroes drove the cars themselves. Bands of whites then began attacking Negro passengers, and there was danger of a race riot. Several Kentucky newspapers and leading citizens of Louisville called for an end to the fighting. Harlan did not duck this hot issue. He denounced the segregation policies of the streetcar company and blamed the violence on Democratic officials' encouragement of anti-Negro extremists. Federal officials backed the Negro ride-ins and threatened court action. Rumors circulated that President Grant planned to send troops to Louisville.

These pressures caused the streetcar company to abandon segregated seating. There was some grumbling by diehards and a few clashes, but within a few weeks, all was quiet on Louisville's streetcars.

Henry Watterson, a young Confederate army veteran and editor of the *Louisville Courier-Journal*, was among those who worked for a peaceful settlement of the ride-in controversy. Earlier, Watterson had shaken up the Democratic party in Kentucky by calling for a "new departure" —a demand that the party stop living in the past and think of the state's future. As a first step he said Democrats should judge a candidate's fitness for office on grounds other than his having served in the Confederate army. He also urged the party to accept the Fourteenth and Fifteenth Amendments, and to back a law allowing Negroes to testify against white men in state courts. Above all, Watterson vigorously opposed the growing spirit of lawlessness that was sweeping Kentucky. He agreed with Harlan that the anti-Klan law passed by Congress was necessary to put an end to night-riding terrorists.

This was strong stuff for die-hard, pro-Confederate Democrats. Led by J. Stoddard Johnston's *Kentucky Yeoman* of Frankfort, they denounced Watterson as an outsider from Tennessee who knew nothing about Kentucky's problems. Watterson persisted and won a strong following throughout the state. The "new departure" Democrats disliked Leslie, whom they accused of being a backward-looking sorehead who wanted to refight the Civil War. But the threat of a Republican victory now served to bring the quarreling Democrats together. They rallied to Leslie in time to give him a 30,000-vote majority over Harlan.

Although he was beaten, Harlan got 63,000 more votes than the Republicans had received in the last state election. Harlan's courageous, forward-looking campaign had put new life into the Republican party in Kentucky. The *Cincinnati Weekly Gazette* insisted that the "election of the entire Republican ticket in almost any other state in the union would have been no greater victory than was won in Kentucky."

During the 1872 presidential campaign, Harlan spoke for Grant in Kentucky and neighboring states. Later

James G. Blaine of Maine, the Speaker of the House of Representatives, asked Harlan and other Republican leaders to come to his state and campaign. Before starting on his speaking tour, Harlan dined at Blaine's home, sitting beside Frederick Douglass, the runaway slave who had become a great abolitionist orator and writer. Harlan traveled with Douglass during the Maine campaign and later told friends: "In my judgment, Douglass had no superior as a public speaker. He would have made a great senator."

The following year, the attorney general of the United States appointed Harlan to "assist in prosecutions for violations" of Negroes' civil rights in Kentucky. While continuing his private law practice, Harlan successfully defended a Negro Methodist congregation when the Southern Methodist Church tried to take over its property.

In 1875, Harlan ran for governor against James Bennett McCreary, a thirty-seven-year-old attorney and former Confederate soldier. Harlan again defended the amendments and laws protecting Negro civil rights against an all-out attack by the Democrats. During one speech Harlan was interrupted by a heckler who asked if it were true that he had sat beside a Negro at a dinner table in Maine. Harlan calmly explained how he happened to sit beside Frederick Douglass. Then he declared, "Fellow citizens, I not only ate beside Douglass at Blaine's house, but I sat at the same table with him in hotels and spoke from the same platform with him. And here let me say that there is no man of any party in Kentucky who can make an abler address . . . than can Frederick Douglass."

The Democrats continued to hammer at Harlan's past record of opposition to civil rights laws. And they warned Kentuckians of the corruption of Radical Republican governments in other states in the South. These appeals to the voters' prejudices and fears were enough to bring the Democrats an easy victory on election day.

10
★
Road to
the Supreme Court

The Republican National Convention of 1876 met in Cincinnati, Ohio, in the middle of June. Harlan led the Kentucky delegation and he nominated his law partner Benjamin H. Bristow for the presidency. There was considerable opposition to Bristow because, according to some, he had been too vigorous in prosecuting dishonest men in the government while he was secretary of the treasury in Grant's first administration. The convention was deadlocked after six ballots and it appeared that Speaker Blaine, whom the Kentucky delegation opposed, might win the nomination. So on the seventh ballot, Harlan withdrew Bristow's name and threw Kentucky's votes to Rutherford B. Hayes, former governor of Ohio. This switch in votes started the drive for Hayes that won him the nomination.

Harlan and Bristow campaigned for the Republican candidates in cities and towns all over Kentucky. The presidential election ended with both sides claiming a victory. The Democratic candidate, Samuel J. Tilden of New York, appeared to have won by a good margin of electoral votes. But the Republicans claimed that there had been fraud in Florida, South Carolina, and Louisiana. They also contested the legality of one electoral vote in Oregon. While an electoral commission of fifteen members studied Democratic and Republican claims, a deal was quietly worked out. The Republicans promised that Hayes would withdraw all federal troops from South Carolina and Louisiana if the Democrats would drop their opposition to Hayes' election. Then the electoral commission ruled for the Republicans in all contests over electoral votes, and Hayes took office in March, 1877. He then withdrew federal troops from South Carolina, and the Republican government in that state collapsed.

The problem in Louisiana required a bit more time to solve. Starting in January, 1877, that state had rival Democratic and Republican governments—two governors, two legislatures, and two sets of courts. Harlan was one of five members of a commission that President Hayes sent to Louisiana to unscramble the mess. (Earlier, Harlan had declined an appointment as ambassador to Britain from the grateful Hayes, who remembered the Kentuckian's aid at the convention.) The commission members spent fifteen days talking with rival officials in Louisiana. Finally the Republican governor, Stephen B. Packard, agreed to take a U.S. consular post in England. This left Democratic Governor Francis T. Nichollas in control of the state-house. Members of the Republican supreme court were also persuaded to resign and take federal jobs elsewhere. On April 21 the commission made its final report, and three days later federal troops left Louisiana. All the former Confederate states once again were controlled by Democrats. As a result the white man in the South was free to handle the Negro problem as he saw fit.

In March, Associate Justice David Davis, who was elected to the Senate, had resigned from the Supreme Court. President Hayes' first choice for the Court post was said to have been Harlan's law partner, Bristow. But there was still opposition to him from Grant's friends and his name was dropped. Then Hayes announced that the name of John Marshall Harlan would be submitted to the Senate. Harlan was, at forty-four, one of the youngest men ever nominated to be an associate justice.

The appointment of Harlan aroused some opposition in the Senate. The leaders of the opposition were Senators Timothy O. Howe of Wisconsin and Isaac Christiancy of Michigan, who had hankered for the appointment themselves. Some senators recalled that Harlan had op-posed Lincoln's policies. Others were suspicious of his proslavery past and doubted his support of Negro civil rights. But after a study of speeches he had made between 1871 and 1877, the Senate finally confirmed his nomination as an associate justice.

Mallie Harlan wrote later that the good news from the Senate had arrived on Thanksgiving Day. She recalled that Harlan, who was restless and worried by the Senate's delay, had finally agreed to go out and play football with his three sons. "When my four boys (for my husband was always a boy along with his three sons) returned, late that afternoon—tired and happy and hungry for their Thanksgiving Dinner—a telegram was waiting for him, informing him that the Senate had . . . confirmed his nomination."

11
★
The Constitution Is
What the Judges Say It Is

Though it is vital to our system of government, the Supreme Court of the United States gets little attention in our Constitution. The Founding Fathers used just sixty-seven words to create the judicial branch of the government:

> The judicial power of the United States shall be vested in one Supreme Court, and in such inferior courts as the Congress may from time to time ordain and establish. The judges, both of the Supreme and inferior courts, shall hold their offices during good behavior, and shall, at stated times, receive for their services a compensation which shall not be diminished during their continuance in office.

No qualifications such as age or residence or citizenship are laid down for judges, as is the case with the president and members of Congress.

Our national court system was established by Congress with the passage of the Judiciary Act of 1789. The first Supreme Court consisted of a chief justice and five associate justices. The number was later increased to a total membership of seven, then to nine, then ten and back to nine. In 1865 Congress enacted a law reducing the membership of the Court to seven to prevent President Johnson from having a chance to nominate anyone. In 1869, after Grant became president, Congress increased the Court's membership to nine, at which number it has remained for 100 years.

Of the "inferior courts," the lowest ranking are the district courts, and there are around 100 today. Above them are the eleven circuit courts of appeals. When Harlan joined the Supreme Court, justices still had the tiring and time-consuming job of traveling twice a year to distant parts of the country to preside over circuit courts of appeals.

The "jurisdiction" of the Supreme Court, which means its right to hear and decide a case, was more carefully spelled out in the Constitution. The Court has original jurisdiction in all cases involving "ambassadors, other public ministers and consuls, and those in which a state shall be a party." That is, such cases are tried exclusively in the Supreme Court. Appellate jurisdiction involves the appeal of a decision from the lower federal or state courts to the Supreme Court, on the ground that a person's rights under the Constitution are involved. It is through the exercise of this appellate jurisdiction that the Supreme Court has come to have the final word on the meaning of certain clauses in the Constitution. The Constitution contains many general clauses such as "due process of law," "privileges and immunities," and "equal protection of the laws." Over the years, justices of the Supreme Court have read into these clauses their own ideas of what they mean. Chief Justice Charles Evans Hughes frankly admitted that "the Constitution is what the judges say it is."

The Constitution and all of its amendments can be read in less than thirty minutes. But it would take a person many years to read carefully the volumes of decisions involving the Constitution that have been handed down by the Supreme Court.

It is not the Supreme Court's job to keep an eye on federal and state courts and correct all the mistakes these courts might make in deciding cases. The Court simply would not have the time to consider the hundreds of cases people would want it to look into. As it is, the Court is busy. (During Harlan's thirty-three years on the Court, he participated in 14,226 cases.)

In deciding which cases to accept, the Court picks those that involve issues affecting a great many people. In addition, the person appealing the case must be in immediate danger of suffering an injury. A decision handed down by the Court on June 9, 1969, illustrates these points. By a seven-to-one vote, the Court declared unconstitutional Wisconsin's wage garnishment law because it permitted a creditor to collect a portion of a person's wages without first proving that a debt really existed. (Garnishment involves the withholding by an employer of a portion of an employee's wages, which is then turned over to a person to whom the employee allegedly owes money.)

The Court's decision left in doubt the legality of garnishment laws in sixteen other states that permit finance companies to freeze a portion of a worker's wages without first granting him a hearing in court. The majority opinion of the Court, which was read by Justice William O. Douglas, stressed the fact that the Wisconsin law did not require the creditor to show that attachment of a person's wages was necessary to collect the debt. Justice Douglas contended that such a law gave creditors the power "to drive a wage-earning family to the wall."

The decision also strengthened a federal law which makes it illegal for an employer to dismiss a worker because his wages are attached by a creditor. Some employers had been avoiding the bookkeeping involved in garnishment deductions by declaring that any worker who had had his wages attached, and who did not clear up the debt, would lose his job.

Clearly, Justice Douglas' opinion is of interest to millions of people, as well as to officials in Wisconsin, and to the sixteen other states whose laws may have to be changed.

The right of the Supreme Court to declare federal and

state laws unconstitutional was stated for the first time by Chief Justice John Marshall in 1803 in *Marbury* v. *Madison*. This power of "judicial review" was not given to the Court by the Constitution, but Marshall argued that since "the Constitution is the supreme law of the land," it is the duty of the Court to declare whether an act of Congress or a state legislature was "repugnant to the Constitution." No other Court in the world has this power of judicial review. The Court has declared few acts of Congress unconstitutional, but one such decision—*Dred Scott* v. *Sandford*—held the Missouri Compromise unconstitutional and all but made the Civil War inevitable. Another, in 1895, involving the income tax, brought a heavy attack upon the Court as a defender of the rich.

12
★
Harlan's Associates

When John Marshall Harlan was sworn in as an associate justice on December 10, 1877, the Supreme Court already was well into its term which had begun in October. He soon became acquainted with the routine of a justice. There were days to hear the arguments of lawyers, and conference days when cases were being decided. Decisions of the Court were announced on Mondays. The chief justice presided at conferences, but he had only one vote and no more power than any other justice on the Court.

Morrison Remick Waite, who became chief justice in 1874, was the fourth man President Grant had selected for the job. The first man he picked declined the honor. The second man, who was Grant's attorney general, had to withdraw when accused of corruption. A third was blocked because of his seventy-four years and charges that he "never allowed principle or conscience to stand in the way of gain." Finally Grant picked Waite, a successful Ohio lawyer, but scarcely known outside his home state.

Newspapers generally greeted the appointment with relief rather than praise. One said: "The President has with remarkable skill avoided choosing any first-rate man. . . . On the whole, considering what the President might have done and tried to do, we ought to be very thankful and give Mr. Waite a cordial welcome."

This was a perfect example of damning a man with faint praise. Waite proved, however, to be an honest, hard-working chief justice.

To the chief justice's right on the bench sat the senior associate justice, Nathan Clifford of Maine, a huge man whose mental powers were rapidly fading. As the only justice appointed by a Democratic president (Buchanan in 1858), Clifford hung on grimly, hoping that another Democrat would be elected so that his successor would also be a Democrat.

Next in seniority on the Court were three members appointed by Lincoln. Noah H. Swayne of Ohio had few qualifications for the job, but he was one of the original members of the Republican party, so he had won the post.

Samuel Freeman Miller of Iowa, Lincoln's second appointee, had started his professional career as a physician, not a lawyer. After ten years of medical practice, he studied law and was admitted to the bar at the age of thirty-one. He was so highly respected in the Midwest that an overwhelming majority of congressmen signed a petition supporting his appointment. During his twenty-eight years on the Court, Miller wrote more opinions than any other justice. Although a great humanitarian who placed the welfare of society ahead of private property and business interests, Miller still was no more liberal than the majority of justices in cases involving Negro civil rights.

The third Lincoln appointee was a Democrat, Stephen Johnson Field of California, one of the most brilliant and colorful of all justices. Two attempts were made on his life after he went to Washington, and he regularly carried a pistol. He served thirty-four years on the Court —longer than any other justice—and well represented the conservative viewpoint on the Court that Harlan and Miller contended against. Field, a stand-pat conservative, felt that the government should not "meddle" with business. Dissenting against a decision upholding a state law regulating business, Field declared: "If this be sound law . . . all property and all business in the state are held at the mercy of the majority of the legislature." This rule of the majority did not disturb Harlan and Miller. They felt that the words "promote the general welfare" in the Preamble to the Constitution should be taken seriously by the government.

This Thomas Nast cartoon in *Harper's Weekly*, September 26, 1868, contended that all Democrats backing Horatio Seymour and Francis P. Blair, Jr. (who opposed the Republican candidates for president and vice-president, General U.S. Grant and Henry Wilson), were in effect Ku Klux Klan members supporting the same cause that the Confederacy had fought for on the field of battle. This was an extreme view, but the anti-Negro raids of the KKK in Kentucky did help to swing John Marshall Harlan over to the Republican party.

John Marshall Harlan (1877 to 1911). His tenure on the Court was exceeded only by those of Justice Field and Chief Justice Marshall.

Henry B. Brown (1891 to 1906). He wrote the majority opinion of the Court upholding the "separate but equal" doctrine in *Plessy v. Ferguson*. This decision prompted Harlan to make his most eloquent dissent.

Samuel F. Miller (1862 to 1890). He switched from medicine to law and became one of the "giants" of the Court. Miller was a foe of special privilege, but no more liberal than a majority of his colleagues regarding the civil rights of Negroes.

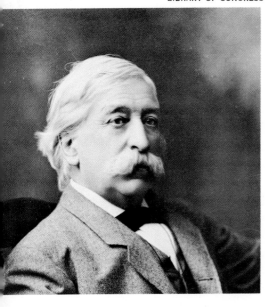

Melville W. Fuller (1888 to 1910). He was so obscure that when he was nominated for chief justice he was called "the man nobody knows." A man who liked peace and quiet, Fuller started the custom that all the justices shake hands before beginning a Court session.

Rufus W. Peckham (1896 to 1909). This big-business lawyer never agreed with Harlan on politics or questions of law, but the two men were good friends outside the Court.

Stephen J. Field (1863 to 1897). Appointed by President Lincoln, this pistol-packing conservative was one of the Court's most brilliant justices. He served longer than any justice before him, including Chief Justice John Marshall.

Horace Gray (1882 to 1892). The nomination of this great legal scholar was strongly urged upon President Chester A. Arthur by Justices Harlan and Miller.

Stanley Matthews (1881 to 1889). The nomination of this railroad lawyer was rejected once by the Senate, but later he was approved by a one-vote margin.

Joseph McKenna (1898 to 1925). His nomination was opposed by many judges and lawyers, but McKenna tended to his "homework" and became a valuable member of the Court.

Oliver Wendell Holmes (1902 to 1932). This brilliant scholar and writer teamed with Harlan to protest the use of "due process" to kill laws opposed by big-business interests.

Next in seniority came Justice William Strong of Pennsylvania, who had been appointed to the Court by Grant in 1870. A former railroad attorney, Strong did nothing on the Court to upset the arch-conservative Justice Field. When Strong resigned in 1880, he wryly explained that he would rather leave and have people say, "Why does he?" than remain until people asked, "Why doesn't he?"

Little had been expected of another railroad lawyer, Joseph P. Bradley of New Jersey, who also was appointed to the Court in 1870. But Bradley proved to be a man of wide interests and education and was one of the best legal scholars on the Court.

A year after Harlan joined the Court, Justice Ward Hunt of New York suffered a stroke and took no part in the Court's work for several years. To get him off the bench, Congress passed a law in 1882 which allowed him to retire on full pay.

When Justice Strong resigned, President Hayes appointed William Burnham Woods, a native of Ohio who had settled in Alabama and then moved to Georgia after he was appointed a circuit court judge by Grant in 1869. He proved to be a below-the-average justice.

In 1881, Stanley Matthews of Ohio replaced Justice Clifford, who finally gave up waiting for a Democrat to be elected president. Matthews had been involved in striking the bargain by which Hayes became president, the promise to withdraw federal troops from the South. Hayes' apparent attempt to reward Matthews ran into rough weather, though. While a member of the Senate, Matthews had vigorously supported bills favoring the railroads and had served as their attorney. These facts caused the Senate to reject his appointment. But when Garfield succeeded Hayes as president in 1881, he reappointed Matthews. The Senate, after a bitter debate, approved Matthews by a one-vote margin.

When Chester Arthur became president after Garfield's assassination in 1881, Justices Harlan and Miller both called upon him to appoint Horace Gray to replace Justice Swayne. Gray was a brilliant legal scholar and chief justice of Massachusetts' Supreme Judicial Court.

Shortly after Harlan took his place on the Supreme Court, Chief Justice Waite expressed his confidence in him. He wrote to a judge on the circuit court of appeals: "Harlan will give entire satisfaction to the public and the profession. He is a worker and will take hold with energy, I am sure. . . . He will be liked both as a judge and as a man."

Harlan plunged into his work with the same energy he had shown during numerous political campaigns in Kentucky. And there was much work to be done. For during the twelve years since the end of the war, the number of cases awaiting action by the Court had been increasing steadily. At the same time, Justice Hunt was ill and Justice Clifford senile. Furthermore, Justice Field was busy campaigning for the Democratic presidential nomination. When he missed the nomination in 1880, he immediately set his sights on the 1884 campaign and paid even less attention to Court business.

When Hunt finally retired in 1882 Samuel Blatchford of New York, who had been a federal district and circuit court judge for fifteen years, was appointed by President Arthur.

There were no changes on the Court from 1882 to 1888, when Chief Justice Waite died, presumably from a combination of too much work on the Court and too many banquets and speeches. In 1887, with the Supreme Court four years behind in its work, Waite had appealed to Congress for "relief for the people against the tedious and oppressive delays of federal justice." Finally in 1891 Congress paid attention to the late chief justice's plea and passed a law giving each circuit court of appeals power to make a final decision in many cases that previously had gone to the Supreme Court. This law also ended the justices' burdensome trips on circuit court duty.

Waite's successor as Chief Justice was Melville W. Fuller of Illinois. He was probably the seventh or eighth man considered for the position by President Grover Cleveland. Opposition by Irish-Americans blocked one candidate. Another lost out when the president said he didn't want to appoint a man who might be arrested by the police some morning. One of the strongest candidates, John Schofield of Illinois, regretfully declined, saying that his wife, who was raised on the frontier, had never learned to wear shoes. Cleveland's advisers agreed that it wouldn't be proper for the wife of the chief justice to go barefoot in Washington.

Melville Fuller, called "the man nobody knows," had been a hard-working lawyer, but a turning point in his plodding career came when he married a banker's daughter. He did legal chores for his father-in-law and worked with the Democratic boss of Chicago, W. C. Goudy. Goudy wanted to be chief justice, but his age and his connections with railroads ruled him out. With reluctance, Goudy finally backed Fuller, and Cleveland appointed him. Fuller also had the support of Justice Harlan, despite the fact that Fuller had opposed Harlan's appointment to the Court. The two men had since become friends, and Harlan's son James had studied law in Fuller's office.

A mild man who liked peace and quiet on the Court, Chief Justice Fuller started the custom whereby all the justices shake hands before they begin a Court session. Fuller seemed to feel that this ceremony might keep some of the hot-tempered justices from coming to blows during arguments over a case.

While the search was on for a chief justice, William B. Woods died after seven little-noticed years on the Court. He was replaced by Lucius Quintus Cincinnatus Lamar, former Confederate colonel, senator from Mississippi, and secretary of the interior.

When Justice Matthews died in 1889, David Josiah

Brewer, a nephew of Justice Field, was appointed to the Court. Brewer had studied law in the office of another uncle, David Dudley Field, one of the nation's outstanding lawyers. Brewer had later served on the Kansas Supreme Court and the federal circuit court of appeals.

Harlan and Brewer became good friends although their political and legal ideas were far apart. Brewer was as stand-pat in his conservatism as his uncle. Joining Justice Field in one dissent, Brewer spurned the notion that government is the "keeper" of the people. "The paternal theory of government to me is odious," he said. "The utmost possible liberty to the individual, and the fullest protection to him and his property, are both the limitation and duty of government."

The great liberal justice Samuel Miller died in 1890. Benjamin Harrison, who had been elected president in 1888, appointed Henry Billings Brown of Michigan to the Court. A successful Detroit lawyer, and a federal judge, Brown was industrious, honest, and pleasant. But he proved no great asset to the Court.

When Justice Bradley died in 1892, President Harrison appointed George Shiras, Jr., of Pittsburgh to fill the empty seat. Shiras was another successful railroad lawyer with no judicial experience. The Senate grumbled, but finally approved him.

After only five years on the Court, Justice Lamar died, and President Harrison appointed Howell E. Jackson, who had earlier urged the president to appoint Justice

Brown. Brown had returned the favor by recommending Jackson. A Tennessee Democrat, Jackson was startled to find himself placed on the Court by a Republican president—the first such appointment since Lincoln appointed Democrat Stephen J. Field in 1863.

The next year, 1894, Justice Blatchford died, and President Grover Cleveland, who had been elected in 1892, appointed Democrat Edward Douglas White. The son of a sugar planter who had been governor of Louisiana, White had served in the Confederate army, become a state senator, a state supreme court judge, and United States senator. Although his appointment to the Court was approved by the Senate on February 19, 1894, White did not resign from that body for two weeks. He stayed on in the Senate to take part in the bitter debate over a sugar bill that he, as a sugar planter, was financially interested in. Even the Democratic *New York World* called White's action "disgraceful," but he ignored all criticism and took his place on the Court. In 1910, after serving as a competent but highly conservative member of the Court, White became chief justice.

Justice Jackson died after only two years on the Court, and President Cleveland appointed Rufus W. Peckham, a New York lawyer and a judge of the New York court of appeals to take his place.

This list of justices covers most of those who served with Harlan during his long career on the Court, particularly during his lone fights for Negroes' civil rights.

13
★
The Civil Rights Cases

A crucial part of the Fourteenth Amendment, which granted the Negro citizenship, was the clause forbidding any state to "deny to any person . . . the equal protection of the laws." In the first case that tested the power and meaning of this clause, the Supreme Court agreed with Congress—and all seemed well for the Negro. This case involved Taylor Strauder, an ex-slave convicted of murder in 1874 in West Virginia. The laws of that state barred Negroes from sitting on a grand jury or trial jury. Strauder's lawyers appealed to the Supreme Court on the ground that racial discrimination denied him the full and equal protection of the laws. The case was decided by the Court in 1880, and Justice Harlan joined the majority in affirming Strauder's right to equal protection. Justice Strong's opinion for the Court declared:

[The Fourteenth Amendment] ordains that no state shall deprive any person of life, liberty or property without due process of law, or deny to any person . . . the equal protection of the laws. What is this but declaring that the law of the states shall be the same for the black as for the white; that all persons, whether colored or white, shall stand equal before the laws of the states, and, in regard to the colored race, for whose protection the amendment was primarily designed, that no discrimination shall be made against them by law because of their color?

There could be no doubt, added Strong, that West Virginia's jury law discriminated against Negroes. Denying men the right to sit on juries because of their color, the justice concluded, put a brand on them marking them as inferiors, and prevented them from securing "that equal justice which the law aims to secure to all others."

If the Supreme Court had followed its decision in *Strauder* v. *West Virginia* in all other civil rights cases, the history of race relations in this country would have been less marked by violence and bitterness. But the Court did not do this. The *Strauder* decision came at a time when United States troops had been withdrawn from the South, and the white man was starting to "solve" the Negro problem in his own way. The Supreme Court soon began to sense that people in the North were getting tired of Radical Republican talk of Negro rights. The country was becoming convinced that the South should be left to handle its own affairs.

Within three years the Supreme Court was to reflect the country's changed mood toward the Negro's dream of equality. During the late 1870's, blacks had begun to seek the protection of the Civil Rights Act of 1875, which required for all races "the full and equal enjoyment of accommodations in inns, theaters . . . and public conveyances on land and water." They went into federal courts in several states, asking that their right to equal treatment be upheld.

Federal district judges in Pennsylvania, Maryland, Texas, and Kentucky ruled that the act was constitutional and they handed down decisions favoring the Negroes. But in North Carolina, New Jersey, and California, federal district judges held the act unconstitutional. Then district courts in New York, Tennessee, Missouri, and Kansas sent cases on to federal circuit courts of appeals. These judges divided on the question, and the issue was sent to the Supreme Court. Two cases testing the act reached the Court in 1876 and a third in 1877, but the justices took no action. In 1880 three more cases reached the Court.

It was not until 1883 that the Court, in the *Civil Rights Cases*, ruled on the legality of the Civil Rights Act of 1875. These cases involved theaters in New York City and San Francisco, a restaurant in Topeka, Kansas, and a hotel in Jefferson City, Missouri, which all refused to admit blacks, and a railroad in Tennessee that refused to seat a black woman in the ladies' car.

On October 15, 1883, Justice Bradley delivered the majority opinion of the Court in the five cases. By an eight-to-one vote, the Court held that the Civil Rights Act of 1875 was unconstitutional. Bradley said that the discriminations complained of actually had nothing to do with slavery. Thus, they could not be forbidden by Congress under the Thirteenth Amendment. "It would," Bradley said, "be running the slavery argument into the ground to make it apply to every act of discrimination which a person may see fit to make as to the guests he will entertain, or as to the people he will take into his coach or cab or car, or admit to his concert or theatre." The justice went on to contend that the denial of equal accommodations did not fix a "badge" of servitude on the colored race.

As for the Fourteenth Amendment, said Bradley, it forbade only *state* actions that deprived a person of his rights. It did not apply to *private* acts of discrimination taken, say, by a hotel or theater owner, against a black person. Such private acts, insisted Bradley, could be prohibited only by state laws, not by Congress. He then concluded that it was time for the Negro to cease being "the special favorite of the law" and become a "mere citizen."

The only dissent came from John Marshall Harlan, the ex-slave owner, who promised to publish his full opinion as soon as possible. Strangely enough all members of the Court majority had made their careers mainly in Northern and Western states, had supported the Union during the war, and had shown no hostility toward blacks. Bradley, who read the majority opinion, had supported Lincoln during the war and firmly backed the Thirteenth and Fourteenth Amendments.

Throughout the rest of October, Harlan worked early and late in his study, trying to write his dissent. He wanted to protest against the false reasoning in the majority opinion and to warn the nation of the trouble the decision could bring, but he couldn't get his words on paper. "It was a trying time for him," his wife commented later. ". . . As much the youngest man on the Court, and standing alone, as he did in regard to a decision which the whole nation was anxiously awaiting, he felt . . . he must speak not only forcibly but wisely."

While Harlan wrote and rewrote, he was disturbed by reports that Negro groups, Republican party leaders, and newspaper editors were promoting him as the "ideal Republican candidate for President in 1884—a man who could win a large following in both the North and South." At a mass meeting of over 3,000 Negroes and whites in Washington Colonel Robert Ingersoll, a famous orator and civil rights champion, and Frederick Douglass denounced the *Civil Rights Cases* decision and praised Harlan to the loud applause of the crowd. Ingersoll said that "from this decision, John M. Harlan had the breadth of brain, the goodness of heart, and the loyalty of logic to dissent. . . . This judge has associated his name with freedom and he will be remembered as long as men are free."

Harlan sought immediately to halt the presidential boom by insisting that he did not want to be "embarrassed by politics." He wrote many of his friends asking them not to work for him, stating that a justice of the Supreme Court should not let political ambitions distract him.

Praising Harlan's refusal to get into politics, *The New York Times* said, "It is to be regretted that a present member, and one of the ablest lawyers on the bench, does not agree with Justice Harlan in thinking that the most commendable ambition a Supreme Court judge can have is not political but judicial." The *Times* was referring to Justice Field's well-known presidential ambitions.

Day after day letters poured in to Harlan, from his son John Maynard Harlan and many associates in both law and politics, urging him to make his forthcoming opinion "powerful" and "uncompromising." Augustus Willson, who had studied law in Harlan's office and had campaigned for him in the 1870's, wrote Harlan that "your dissent will not be for a section or a race. It will be for the American people . . . and it will be for humanity. Lay it deep and honest and in mortal earnest . . . and, under God, it will yet be the law of the land and a pattern for all nations."

On a Sunday morning early in November when the discouraged Harlan, his opinion still unwritten, had gone to church, his wife had an inspiration. She remembered an inkstand that Chief Justice Taney had used to write all his opinions, and which had been given to Harlan by the marshal of the Supreme Court in 1877. Mallie rummaged around till she found the inkstand; then she cleaned it up, filled it with ink, and put it on her husband's desk. When Harlan returned home and found the inkstand, which he thought had been lost, he had a burst of fresh energy and inspiration. As Mallie Harlan said later, "The memory of the historic part that Taney's inkstand had played in the Dred Scott decision, in temporarily tightening the shackles of slavery upon the Negro race . . . seemed to act like magic in clarifying my husband's thoughts. . . . His pen fairly flew on that day and . . . he soon finished his dissent."

Harlan's published dissent bluntly accused the Court majority of quibbling over the meaning and purpose of the Thirteenth and Fourteenth Amendments. He insisted that the Thirteenth Amendment not only prohibited slavery but gave Congress the power to pass laws forbidding racial discrimination that tended to fix the badge of slavery on a black person. "Was nothing more intended," he asked, "than to forbid one man from owning another as property? Were the states, against whose protest the institution [slavery] was destroyed, to be left free . . . to make or allow discriminations against that race, as such, in the enjoyment of those fundamental rights which . . . inhere in a state of freedom?"

Answering that question with a sharp no, Harlan said: "I hold that since slavery . . . was the moving or principal cause of the adoption of the amendment, and since that institution rested wholly upon the inferiority, as a race, of those held in bondage, their freedom necessarily involved immunity from, and protection against, all discriminations against them, because of their race, in respect of such civil rights as belong to freemen of other races."

Harlan then attacked Bradley's argument that Congress had no power under the Constitution to forbid private acts of discrimination. He sharply reminded his colleagues that Congress had, in 1793 and 1850, passed fugitive slave laws to punish the private acts of persons who aided runaway slaves. These laws, said Harlan, had been ruled constitutional by the Supreme Court. If, he asked, Congress can pass laws protecting a slaveholder against the private acts of persons aiding slaves, why can't it pass laws protecting freed slaves from the private acts of persons who deny them equal rights? "I insist," said Harlan, "that the National Legislature may . . . do for human liberty . . . what it did . . . for the protection of slavery and the rights of the masters of fugitive slaves."

Having thus slashed at Bradley's contention that private acts of discrimination were not covered by the Fourteenth Amendment, Harlan contended that "railroad corporations, keepers of inns and managers of places of public accommodation are agents . . . of the state." As for places of amusement, Harlan pointed out that "the authority to establish and maintain them comes from the public. The colored race is part of that public . . ." and, he went on to explain, is entitled to equal treatment in such places.

Bradley's comment that the Negro had been made "the special favorite of the law" drew a sharp retort from Harlan. He insisted that the Thirteenth and Fourteenth Amendments had been passed not to "favor" blacks but to include them as "part of the people" whose welfare had to be considered. "Today," said Harlan, "it is the colored race which is denied, by corporations and individuals wielding public authority, rights fundamental in their freedom and citizenship. At some future time, it may be that some other race will fall under the ban of race discrimination. If the constitutional amendments be enforced, according to the intent with which, as I conceive, they were adopted, there cannot be in this republic, any class of human beings in practical subjection to another class, with power in the latter to dole out to the former just such privileges as they may choose to grant."

While the majority of the Court and the American people seemed to be forgetting it, Harlan held stubbornly to the purpose of the Thirteenth and Fourteenth Amendments. After opposing them for years as a politician in Kentucky, Harlan had reached the conclusion that these amendments were vital to keep "white supremacy" rabble-rousers in check. Now Harlan protested in vain as the Court told the Negro that he had to look to the states for protection against discrimination. And the states were in no mood to give him protection. In fact, the Supreme Court decision of 1883 encouraged a drive throughout the South to segregate black from white. Blacks were barred from white restaurants and hotels, pushed into filthy Jim Crow railroad cars, given sub-standard separate schooling or none at all, crowded into shanty towns and forced to accept manual labor in cities, or work as sharecroppers on land they did not own. In the North and West, blacks also faced discrimination. They were barred from many restaurants and hotels and theaters. Often they had to accept the poorest housing and ramshackle schools. Labor unions excluded them, denying them the chance to rise above the job of day laborer or house servant.

Harlan's was a voice crying into a rising wind of preju-dice against the Negro. This prejudice was all the more deadly because it was defended as sweetly reasonable by influential editors in the North. "The fact is, and the sooner the fact is recognized the sooner we shall be rid of many dangerous illusions," wrote Richard Watson Gilder in *Century* magazine, "that the negroes constitute a peasantry wholly untrained in, and ignorant of, those ideas of constitutional liberty and progress which are the birthright of every white voter; that they are gregarious and emotional rather than intelligent, and are easily led in any direction by white men of energy and determina-tion."

Turning his back on the Negro's desperate struggle for equality, Edwin L. Godkin wrote in the *Nation*: "I do not see . . . how the negro is ever to be worked into a system of government for which you and I would have much respect."

Harlan, who had held similar ideas as a young man, was to argue without success for the next twenty-five years that the salvation of the nation could come only if all people enjoyed the full rights of citizenship.

14

★

Defender of the
Fourteenth Amendment

John Marshall Harlan's lone dissent in the *Civil Rights
Cases* turned him into a sort of one-man committee to
protect and defend the Fourteenth Amendment—and,
in turn, to use it to protect and defend the rights of all
citizens. In doing so, Harlan stubbornly insisted, year
after year, that the Fourteenth Amendment had increased
the importance of a citizen's relation to the federal government and had reduced the authority of the states. This
amendment, he argued, had extended the freedoms of the
United States Bill of Rights to the citizens of all of the
states.

The first eight amendments, which, properly speaking,
are the Bill of Rights, were approved by Congress in
1791. They sought to protect the personal freedoms of
United States citizens from attack by the federal government, not the states.

The First Amendment safeguards freedom of religion, press, speech, assembly, and petition. The Second guarantees the right of a citizen to bear arms and of a state to have a militia. The Third prevents the quartering of troops in a citizen's home in time of peace. This amendment sounds old-fashioned today, but it was looked upon as vital to the men who fought the Revolution and opposed England's practice of "quartering" troops in private homes.

The Fourth Amendment protects one's home against unreasonable searches and seizures by officers who have no search warrant. Before the Revolution, English officers had "writs of assistance" which allowed them to ransack any and all homes at will.

The Fifth, Sixth, Seventh, and Eighth Amendments protect a person's liberty and property and guarantee him a fair trial. Among the rights guaranteed are: in a criminal case, the right to indictment by a grand jury and a "speedy and public" trial by a jury drawn from the community; the privilege against self-incrimination and double jeopardy (a person cannot be tried twice for the same crime if once found not guilty); the right to be secure from "cruel and unusual punishment." In addition, the Fifth Amendment provides that no person can "be deprived of life, liberty, or property, without due process of law"; nor can private property "be taken for public use without just compensation."

Under our federal system of government, a person has

dual citizenship. He is both a United States citizen and a citizen of the state in which he lives. The rights of a United States citizen are protected by the Bill of Rights. The state constitutions also have "bills of rights" to protect their citizens. Early in our history, however, the question arose: "Does the United States Bill of Rights protect a U.S. citizen from an unfair act by the state in which he lives?" In the case of *Barron* v. *Baltimore* in 1833, the Court held that the Fifth Amendment of the Bill of Rights restricted only the federal government, not the state government. Then in 1868 the Fourteenth Amendment was ratified by the necessary three-fourths of the states. This amendment declared in part: "No state shall make or enforce any law which shall abridge the privileges or immunities of citizens of the United States; nor shall any state deprive any person of life, liberty, or property, without due process of law." This clause appeared to extend the protection of the Fifth Amendment of the Bill of Rights to the citizens of a state.

But the first attempt by residents of a state to seek the protection of the Fourteenth and Fifth Amendments was turned down by the Supreme Court in the *Slaughterhouse Cases* in 1873. An association of New Orleans butchers attacked a state law that granted one company a monopoly to slaughter livestock in New Orleans. Louisiana officials contended that this law was a proper exercise of the state's police power for the protection of the health and comfort of the people. The state maintained that the company enjoying the monopoly operated cleaner slaughterhouses and that the rates it charged butchers were strictly regulated.

The butchers argued that this monopoly denied them their privileges and immunities as citizens of the United States and deprived them of liberty and property without due process of law, and therefore was in violation of the Fourteenth Amendment.

In a five-to-four decision, the Court upheld the Louisiana law. In his opinion for the Court majority, Justice Miller declared that the citizens of a state were given no added protection by the Fourteenth Amendment. Miller added that only the "privileges and immunities" of a U.S. citizen were protected by this amendment, and the right to engage in the slaughterhouse business was not a privilege of U.S. citizenship. The Fourteenth Amendment, Miller concluded, was intended to protect the Negro, not a businessman. But in saying that the citizen of a state was given no added protection by the Fourteenth Amendment, Miller actually took away the Negro's right to equality. This was what happened in the *Civil Rights Cases* when the Court ruled that Congress had no power under the Fourteenth Amendment to protect the civil rights of blacks.

A year after the *Civil Rights Cases*, Harlan's voice was raised again in defense of the Fourteenth Amendment. This case involved the Fifth Amendment requirement that a person can be tried for a serious crime only after indictment by a grand jury. The California constitution had been amended to allow a trial after the accused had been questioned by a magistrate.

In a California court, Joseph Hurtado was accused of murder without a grand jury indictment. He was tried, convicted, and sentenced to death. His lawyer appealed to the Supreme Court on the ground that trial without indictment by a grand jury was prohibited by the Fifth and Fourteenth Amendments, and thus Hurtado would be deprived of life without "due process of law."

Speaking for the Court majority in *Hurtado* v. *California*, Justice Matthews rejected Hurtado's appeal. He contended that certain of the liberties listed in the Bill of Rights, such as grand jury indictment, were not essential to due process of law as guaranteed in the Fourteenth Amendment. Thus, Hurtado was not deprived of any constitutional right and must die on the gallows. In summing up, Matthews did say that due process included "those fundamental principles of liberty and justice which lie at the basis of our civil and political institutions."

Matthews' off-hand statement, in an opinion that had sent a man to his death, aroused Harlan's anger. In his lone dissent, he tartly asked why these rights, such as grand jury indictment, were included in the Bill of Rights if they were not considered fundamental in protecting a person's right to a fair trial. Harlan went on to argue that the "due process" clause came from the laws and customs of England. It meant, he said, "a fair trial," and a most important part of a fair trial was the requirement that no person could be tried for his life without an indictment by a grand jury.

The Supreme Court, said Harlan, had ignored English custom and American practice and had ruled that the due process clause of the Fourteenth Amendment did not require a grand jury indictment in a trial in a state court. The next step, Harlan warned, would be Court decisions holding that due process did not forbid compulsory self-incrimination, cruel and unusual punishment, and trial by a jury of less than twelve persons. All these and other rights to a fair trial, insisted Harlan, had been specifically mentioned in the Bill of Rights because they were considered as "essential to the safety of the people."

According to the majority of the Supreme Court, the states were expected to watch over a citizen's rights. But Harlan asked the common-sense question: who watches the watchmen? Harlan believed that, under the Constitution, this was the job of the Supreme Court. Harlan could not see why a citizen of a state had fewer rights in a state court than he would have if he were in a federal court. He was years ahead of his time in insisting that the due process clause of the Fourteenth Amendment extended the protection of the Bill of Rights to the citizens of a state and restricted a state's power to invade a citizen's rights.

It was not many years before Harlan's warnings in the *Hurtado* case became hard facts of life to citizens accused of crimes. Year after year, the Supreme Court handed down decisions that nibbled away at the Fourteenth Amendment. One of these cases was *O'Neil* v. *Vermont* in 1892. John O'Neil of New York was arrested and tried by a Vermont justice of the peace on a charge of unlawfully selling liquor in that state. He was found guilty of making 457 sales, was fined $9,140, and sentenced to *seventy-nine years* in prison. He appealed the case, and a county court jury reduced his punishment to a fine of $6,140 and *only* fifty-four years in prison. The Vermont supreme court rejected O'Neil's plea that fifty-four years' imprisonment was "cruel and unusual punishment," prohibited by the state constitution. The United States Supreme Court refused to aid O'Neil. It ruled that he had not presented convincing arguments that his crime involved interstate commerce, which is the business of the federal government, not the states. Furthermore, the Court majority refused to even discuss the question of cruel and unusual punishment. It contended that the Eighth Amendment of the Bill of Rights did not apply to the states.

In an angry dissent, Justice Field declared that fifty-four years' imprisonment was a punishment at which "no man of right feeling and heart can refrain from shuddering." He agreed that the Eighth Amendment, forbidding cruel and unusual punishment, formerly was directed only at the federal government. But he reminded the Court majority that this amendment had been given broader coverage by the Fourteenth Amendment, which said that "no state shall make or enforce any law which shall abridge the privileges or immunities of citizens of the United States."

Justice Harlan had not often agreed with the conservative, short-tempered Field. But this time, the Kentuckian gave him strong support. "I fully concur with Mr. Justice Field that since the adoption of the Fourteenth Amendment, no one of the fundamental rights of life, liberty or property, recognized and guaranteed in the Constitution of the United States, can be denied or abridged by a state."

But in 1900, in the case of *Maxwell* v. *Dow*, the Supreme Court again nibbled away at the Fourteenth Amendment. A citizen of Utah named Maxwell had been tried, convicted of robbery by a jury of *eight* persons, and sentenced to eighteen years in prison. His case was appealed to the Supreme Court on the argument that trial by a jury of less than twelve persons deprived him of the privileges and immunities secured to him by the Constitution of the United States and the Fourteenth Amendment.

The Court majority ruled that the right to be tried by a jury of twelve persons, in a case not involving the death penalty, was not a privilege or immunity granted the citizen of a state under the Fourteenth Amendment.

Justice Peckham, in his majority opinion, nailed the case down, at least to his satisfaction, by citing *Hurtado* v. *California* as proof that Maxwell was not deprived of his liberty without due process of law. According to Peckham, the citizen of a state must still look to his state for protection, not to the U.S. Bill of Rights or the Fourteenth Amendment.

Mention of the *Hurtado* case aroused Harlan's ire. In his lone dissent, he said, "It does not solve the question before us to say that the [Bill of Rights] had reference only to the powers of the national government and not to the states." He recalled that before the Fourteenth Amendment was passed, a citizen of the United States could not be tried for a crime except by a jury of twelve persons. He then asked, "How can it be that a citizen of the United States may now be tried in a state court . . . by eight jurors, when the Fourteenth Amendment expressly declares that 'no state shall make or enforce any law which shall abridge the privileges and immunities of citizens of the United States'?"

Harlan concluded his dissent with a warning. "The decision today rendered is very far-reaching in its consequences. I take it no one doubts that the great men who laid the foundations of our government regarded the preservation of the privileges and immunities specified in the [Bill of Rights] as vital to the personal security of American citizens. To say of any people that they do not enjoy those privileges and immunities is to say that they do *not* enjoy real freedom." In view of the present decision, Harlan protested, "the Constitution of the United States does not stand in the way of any state striking down guarantees of life and liberty that English-speaking people have for centuries regarded as vital to personal security, and which the men of the revolutionary period universally claimed as the birthright of freemen."

To Harlan, the principles of the Bill of Rights were sacred elements of liberty, and he strongly opposed any decision that allowed the states to weaken this defense of a citizen's rights. Nor did he think that any citizen should take lightly the rights granted him by the Constitution. In the case of *Schick* v. *United States*, for example, a man had waived his right to trial by jury in a minor matter. Harlan grimly dissented. He argued that no citizen should give up *any* right due him regardless of how trivial his involvement was with the law.

15

★

I Regard This
Decision As a Disaster

One of Harlan's most violent disagreements with the majority of the Supreme Court came in 1895. During President Cleveland's second administration, Congress enacted a bill that put a two percent tax on incomes above $4,000 a year. This tax was defended as a measure to aid the victims of the panic of 1893, which had thrown several million men out of work, by placing the tax burden on the well-to-do. An income tax had been in force during the Civil War, and no attacks had been made on its constitutionality at the time. But when a stockholder in the Farmers' Loan and Trust Company sued to keep the bank from paying a tax on the company's income, big business interests felt that at last there were enough conservatives on the Court to give them a chance of victory. The bank's lawyers were joined by the attorney general of the United States in defending the tax. The stockholder, named Pollock, was represented by a group of big-business lawyers headed by Joseph H. Choate.

Pollock's lawyers called the tax an assault on thrift by the disrupters of society. Joseph Choate warned that if the Court approved the law, along with "its [unfair] exemption of four thousand dollars, then the communistic march goes on. . . . If it is true that the passions of the people are aroused on this subject; if it is true that a mighty army of 60,000,000 citizens is likely to be incensed by this decision, it is the more vital to the future welfare of this country that this Court again resolutely and courageously declare that it *has* the power to set aside an act of Congress violative of the Constitution."

Five justices accepted Choate's challenge to set aside the tax. Speaking for the majority, Chief Justice Fuller held the income tax unconstitutional. He said that under the Constitution all taxes must be uniform; everyone must pay the same amount, as in the case of a poll tax. The government, said Fuller, could not require the rich to pay high taxes and the poor no taxes at all.

While Fuller droned out his opinion, Harlan moved restlessly on the bench and had trouble keeping quiet. He glared at his colleagues and lifted his eyebrows in evident disbelief. Justice Field leaned back contentedly, and Justice Gray's face showed satisfaction.

Then, it was Harlan's turn, and his voice boomed through the courtroom. As he spoke, his fist hammered the bench. Whenever he made an important point, he would turn and defiantly face the chief justice or wave his finger at Justice Field. "This decision," Harlan thundered, "may well excite the gravest apprehension. . . . No tax is more just in its essence than an income tax. . . . On my conscience, I regard this decision as a disaster."

Taking a poke at Choate and other alarmists, Harlan declared emphatically: "It was said in argument that the passage of the statute imposing this income tax was an assault by the poor upon the rich, and by much eloquent speech this court has been urged to stand in the breech for the protection of the just rights of property against the advancing hosts of Socialism. With the policy of legislation of this character the Court has nothing to do. This is for the legislative branch of the government. . . . We deal here only with questions of law." Harlan was reminding certain justices that the Supreme Court had no business meddling in Congress' business, which was the writing of the laws.

Summing up his dissent, Harlan said the majority opinion gave men of wealth too much power over the common people: "The practical effect of the decision is to give to certain kinds of property a position of favoritism and advantage inconsistent with the fundamental principles of our social organization, and to invest them with power and influence that may be perilous to that portion of the American people upon whom rests the larger part of the burdens of government, and who ought not to be subjected to the dominion of aggregated wealth any more than the property of the country should be at the mercy of the lawless."

As expected, Justice Field supported Fuller with a fiery opinion that made Choate happy: "The present assault on capital is but the beginning. It will be but the stepping-stone to others, larger and more sweeping, till our political contests will become a war of the poor against the rich; a war constantly growing in intensity and bitterness. If the Court sanctions the power of discriminating taxation, and nullifies the uniformity mandate of the Constitution, it will mark the hour when the sure decadence of our government will commence."

Dissenting opinions were also read by Justices Brown, White, and Jackson (who died shortly after the Pollock decision) . In his opinion Jackson declared, "The practical operation of the decision is not only to disregard the great principle of equality in taxation, but [also to disregard] the further principle that, in the imposition of taxes for the benefit of the government, the burden thereof should be imposed upon those having most ability to bear them. This decision in effect works out a directly opposite result. . . . It is in my judgment, the most disastrous blow ever struck at the constitutional power of Congress."

Speaking later of the majority opinion that the rich and the poor must be taxed equally, Harlan said disgustedly: "If that is the Constitution, it cannot be amended too quickly." Chief Justice Fuller ran into almost as much abuse as Taney had after his *Dred Scott* decision. Even the most conservative lawyers were amazed by the decision. The *American Law Review* echoed Harlan's dissent and accused the Court of trying to take over Congress' job of law-making. "Some of the judges . . . seem to have no adequate idea of the dividing line between judicial and legislative power, and seem to be incapable of restraining themselves to the mere office of judge."

Eventually Congress began the slow process of amending the Constitution. But before the Sixteenth Amendment, which permitted an income tax, was ratified by the states in 1913, the government lost millions of dollars in taxes not collected.

16

★

Last of the
Tobacco-Spittin' Judges

Good humored and sociable, Harlan limited his disagreements to the conference room and the bench. He enjoyed whist parties with his fellow justices, and was quite fond of Justice Peckham, though they disagreed on politics and questions of law. One day, Harlan told Peckham he would be absent from the Court to attend a church conference. Peckham said in mock seriousness: "You are such a good Presbyterian, Harlan, I don't see why you are afraid to die."

Just as mockingly serious, Harlan said: "I am not if I were sure that in the next world I wouldn't turn up at Democratic headquarters."

Harlan's muscular, erect, six-foot-two-inch frame made him an unforgettable sight on the bench or in a drawing room. His sharp features and massive, bare head gave him the look of a bald eagle—"a compelling presence," said one reporter. His courtly manners made him a life-long favorite of Washington society. Augustus Willson said of him: "He had a genuine, great-hearted sense of humor and was always a delightful host and a joyful guest."

In 1889 Justice Harlan joined the faculty of the Columbian (now George Washington) University School of Law. From that time until the year of his death, he lectured on constitutional law. Easy-going and plain-spoken, he was popular with his students. One day, when he completed a rousing lecture on a constitutional question, his students applauded. Embarrassed, Harlan gently chided them: "Come, come. I was not delivering a political speech."

Each day Harlan rode the back platform of a street-car to work. There he was ready to discuss the news with any passenger. Every morning he bought his news-paper from the same aged vendor. If this man was not at his post, Harlan would disconsolately pass on, refusing to patronize any other dealer. Every noon the justice usually had a glass of milk and a piece of pie at a low-priced restaurant.

Justice Oliver Wendell Holmes called Harlan "the last of the tobacco-spittin' judges." Harlan's fondness for tobacco became widely known during hearings on a tobacco company case. He remarked to an attorney that it was hard to get tobacco that was not adulterated or spoiled. Newspapers quoted this remark, and the startled Harlan soon received presents of tobacco from all over the country.

After the death of Justice Miller in 1890, Harlan was next to Justice Field in seniority on the Court. Unlike Field, who was showing signs of senility, Harlan was in excellent health and he remained the hardest working member of the Court. Field hung on though, determined to set the record for years of service. Finally, several justices persuaded the reluctant Harlan to talk to Field about resigning. Gently, Harlan asked Field if he remembered many years before when he had been on a committee that asked a senile justice to resign. Field listened quietly. Then, eyes blazing, he snarled, "Yes, and a dirtier day's work I never did in my life!" No further attempts were made to force Field's retirement. At last in April of 1897, Field sent in his resignation, specifying that it would not take effect until December. This delay permitted Field to serve on the Court longer than any other justice had before him.

The appointment of a justice to replace Field aroused considerable controversy. President McKinley, who had taken office that year, proposed the name of Joseph McKenna. He had been a California state legislator, a federal circuit court judge, a member of Congress, and was attorney general in McKinley's cabinet. McKenna's appointment was opposed by one federal judge who said he was sloppy, inefficient, and behind in his work when

he was a circuit court judge. Another jurist said Mc-
Kenna's "unfitness for a judicial office is glaring and
well known." A group of leading West Coast lawyers
called McKenna's record on the bench "disgraceful."
The Senate listened to all the protests and then approved
the appointment. It seemed to feel that McKenna, who
was only fifty-five, might prove more efficient than some
of the other respected members of the Court. It was
well-known that Gray and Shiras, both ill, often fell
asleep on the bench. During his twenty-seven years on
the Court, McKenna worked hard and became a fairly
effective judge. Some of his opinions were as far-sighted
as those of Harlan or Miller. In the past, appointment
to the Court had often made a man rise to the challenge
of his important post. This certainly happened in the case
of McKenna.

On December 9, 1902, a group of lawyers who tried
cases before the Supreme Court gave Harlan a dinner
celebrating his twenty-fifth year of service. President Theodore Roosevelt was there to open the dinner and, as he
said, "to do homage to a career which has honored
America." Then, after telling the assembled guests that
he didn't believe in making after-dinner speeches, Chief
Justice Fuller called on Harlan's good friend Justice
Brewer to deliver the main address.

When not complaining of some law that "meddled"
with business, Brewer displayed a ready wit and a deft way
of poking fun at his colleagues. "It is a difficult task,"

he said, "to speak for a body like the Supreme Court, each one of whose members is so conscious of his ability to speak for himself. You will readily perceive this should you come to the courtroom on a Monday morning and listen to his attempted explanation of his own opinion."

Turning with a smile toward Harlan, Brewer said: "I cannot decline to say a few words in honor of one with whom, for thirteen years, I have had my earnest controversies over the Constitution and the law, yet never a harsh or unkindly word. The brevity of the notice given me only this morning [to make this speech] is an assurance that my talk will not be long—no longer than one of Brother Harlan's dissents and perhaps no better.

"To sit in the conference room of the Supreme Court and struggle with Mr. Justice Harlan in the consideration of the various cases presented is of itself a legal education, at least to any one capable of receiving such an education. I regret that my juvenile brethren seem to have profited so little by this and other instructions."

Concluding, Brewer said of Harlan, "He goes to bed every night with one hand on the Constitution and the other on the Bible, and so sleeps the sweet sleep of justice and righteousness. He believes in the Constitution as it was written . . . and the Constitution as it shall be, unless and until the American people shall, in the way they have appointed, amend its provisions."

When Harlan was seventy-five the members of the Supreme Court challenged the younger members of the

Washington bar to a baseball game. When his turn at bat came, Harlan stepped to the plate, took a healthy swing, and sent the ball to deepest centerfield. The justice, his huge figure erect and his coattails flying, reached third base before the ball was thrown in.

17
★
The Constitution
Is Color-Blind

One year after the 1895 income tax case Harlan was fighting alone again, this time to defend the Negroes' right to the "equal protection of the laws." After the 1883 Supreme Court decision in the *Civil Rights Cases*, Florida, Alabama, Arkansas, Georgia, and Tennessee passed laws requiring railroads to separate white and Negro passengers. Then on July 10, 1890, the Louisiana General Assembly passed and the governor signed "an act to promote the comfort of passengers" in railroad cars. It required the railroads "to provide equal but separate accommodations for the white and colored races."

The law was denounced by a Negro organization, the American Citizens' Equal Rights Association of Louisiana Against Class Legislation. It said the measure would "be

119

a free license to the evilly-disposed that they might with impunity insult, humiliate, and otherwise maltreat inoffensive persons, and especially women and children who should happen to have a dark skin."

One member of the association, L. A. Martinet, editor of the *New Orleans Crusader*, announced: "The bill is now law. The next thing is what are we going to do?" Martinet and R. L. Desdunes then led in forming the Citizens Committee to Test the Constitutionality of the Separate Car Law. Money was raised to finance the case, and Martinet hired a lawyer, Albion W. Tourgée of Mayville, New York. Before moving north, Tourgée had been an officer in the Union army and had practiced law in Greensboro, North Carolina, after the war. A leader in the Radical Republican party there, he helped write the new state constitution and later served as a judge on the superior court of North Carolina. Martinet explained to Tourgée that railroad officials "want to help us but dread public opinion." The officials felt that the law was a nuisance and "a bad and mean one." Tourgée conferred with Martinet and others and picked a person to test the legality of the law.

On a June day in 1892 Homer Adolph Plessy boarded a car of the East Louisiana Railroad in New Orleans to travel to Covington, Louisiana. Plessy was one-eighth Negro—one of his eight great-grandparents had been of African descent. He entered a car reserved for whites, and when he refused to leave, a railroad detective arrested him. Plessy's case became *Plessy* v. *Ferguson* when Judge John H. Ferguson of the Criminal District Court of New Orleans overruled Tourgée's plea that the separate-car law violated the Constitution of the United States. Tourgée then appealed to the Louisiana Supreme Court, which upheld the law. But the state's chief justice did grant Tourgée a writ permitting him to take the case to the United States Supreme Court.

In his argument before the Supreme Court, Tourgée contended that the clue to the true intent of the Louisiana law was that it did not apply to "[colored] nurses attending the children of the other race." Said Tourgée: "The exemption of nurses shows that the real evil lies not in color of the skin but in the relation the colored person sustains to the white. If he is dependent, it may be endured; if he is not, his presence is insufferable. Instead of being intended to promote the general comfort and moral well-being, this act is plainly and evidently intended to promote the happiness of one class by asserting its supremacy and the inferiority of another class. Justice is pictured as blind, and her daughter, the law, ought at least to be color-blind."

Seven members of the Supreme Court (one did not take part in the case) ruled against Plessy. The majority opinion, read by Justice Henry B. Brown, rejected the argument that "the enforced separation of the races stamps the colored race with the badge of inferiority. If this be so, it is not by reason of anything found in the act, but solely because the colored race chooses to put that construction upon it."

Without coming right out and saying so, Justice Brown strongly hinted that laws that separated the races were desirable and necessary. "In determining reasonableness [the legislature] is at liberty to act with reference to established usages, customs and traditions of the people." (In other words, if whites are used to discriminating against blacks, it is all right for the legislature to pass a law making this discrimination easier.)

Defending this line of thought, Brown continued: "If the civil and political rights of both races be equal, one cannot be inferior to the other civilly or politically. If one race is inferior to the other socially, the Constitution . . . cannot put them on the same plane."

However, Justice Brown carefully avoided answering the obvious question, "How can there be civil and political equality when the Negro is barred from voting and is fenced away from whites with Jim Crow laws?"

Harlan's powerful dissent—it was his greatest one—took up this question and pounded at Brown's attempt to establish white supremacy in the nation. "The white race," Harlan said, "deems itself to be the dominant race in this country. And so it is, in prestige, in achievements, in education, in wealth, and in power. So, I doubt not, it will continue for all time, if it remains true to its great heritage and holds fast to the principles of constitutional liberty. But in the view of the Constitution, in the eye of the law, there is in this country no superior, dominant ruling class of citizens. There is no caste here. Our Constitution is color-blind, and neither knows nor tolerates classes among citizens. In respect of civil rights, all citizens are equal before the law. The humblest is the peer of the most powerful. The law regards man as man, and takes no account of his surroundings or of his color when his civil rights, as guaranteed by the supreme law of the land, are involved. It is, therefore, to be regretted that this high tribunal . . . has reached the conclusion that it is competent for a state to regulate the enjoyment by citizens of their civil rights solely upon the basis of race."

Taking dead aim at the Louisiana law, Harlan thundered: "The destinies of the two races in this country are indissolubly linked together, and the interests of both require that the common government of all shall not permit the seeds of race hate to be planted under the sanction of law. What can more certainly arouse race hatred, what more certainly create and perpetuate a feeling of distrust between these races, than state enactments, which, in fact, proceed on the ground that colored citizens are so inferior and degraded that they cannot be allowed to sit in public coaches occupied by white citizens? That, as all will admit, is the real meaning of such legislation as was enacted in Louisiana."

Recalling another time when the Court drew a color

line through the nation, Harlan said: "In my opinion, the judgment this day rendered will, in time, prove to be quite as pernicious as the decision made by this tribunal in the Dred Scott case. It was adjudged in that case that the descendants of Africans . . . were not included nor intended to be included under the word 'citizens' in the Constitution. . . . The recent amendments to the Constitution, it was supposed, have eradicated these principles from our institutions. But it seems that we have yet, in some states, a dominant race, a superior class of citizens, which assumes to regulate the enjoyment of civil rights, common to all citizens, on the basis of race. The present decision, it may be apprehended, will not only stimulate aggressions, more or less brutal and irritating, upon the admitted rights of colored citizens, but will encourage the belief that it is possible, by means of state enactments, to defeat the beneficent purposes which the people of the United States had in view when they adopted the recent amendments to the Constitution."

Concluding his impassioned dissent, Harlan looked ahead and laid down a pattern of conduct that, if followed, would have done much to insure racial peace and justice in the nation.

The sure guarantee of the peace and security of each race is the clear and distinct, unconditional recognition by our governments, National and State, of every right that inheres in civil freedom, and of the equality before the law of all citizens . . . without regard to race. State enactments, regulating the enjoyment of civil rights, upon the basis of race, and cunningly devised to defeat the legitimate results of the war, under the pretense of recognizing equality of rights, can have no other result than to render permanent peace impossible, and to keep alive a conflict of races, the continuance of which must do harm to all concerned. . . .

If evils result from the commingling of the two races upon public highways established for the benefit of all, they will be infinitely less than those that will surely come from state legislation regulating the enjoyment of civil rights upon the basis of race. We boast of the freedom enjoyed by our people above all other peoples. But it is difficult to reconcile that boast with a state of the law which, practically, puts the brand of servitude and degradation upon a large class of our fellow citizens, our equals before the law. The thin disguise of "equal" accommodations for passengers in railroad coaches will not mislead any one, or atone for the wrong this day done.

Unfortunately Harlan's common-sense warning was ignored. Few people cared to note that the Negro now was in a "no-man's land." In the *Civil Rights Cases*, the Court had denied Congress the power to protect the rights of the colored race. Then in *Plessy* v. *Ferguson*, the Court upheld a state law denying the race equal treatment. As a result of the two rulings, Congress was prevented from helping the Negro, and the states were encouraged to fix the badge of inferiority on him.

18

★

Rise of the Trusts

In the America of the 1870's and 1880's, people believed that free competition was best for business and its customers. Congress' main job was to keep tariffs high enough to protect American business from low-priced foreign goods and to encourage the building of railroads that would help the farmers and businessmen move their goods to market.

But as businesses—steel, oil, meat packing, sugar refining, railroads—began to grow and become nationwide, the fight for customers became rougher. In the 1880's, for example, five railroads were competing for business between New York and Chicago, and two more railroads were under construction. The competition became so cutthroat that the railroad fare between New York and Chicago was beaten down to $1. The oil industry also suffered from the same savage competition in the 1870's and many companies failed.

Seeking a way to limit competition and protect their profits, businessmen began forming "pools," secret agreements to fix prices and share markets. A leader in such agreements was John D. Rockefeller. His Standard Oil Company and several other firms formed an association called the South Improvement Company in the late 1870's. This combination was strong enough to force railroads to carry members' oil at lower rates than those charged competing oil companies. South Improvement also forced the railroads to secretly give it part of the freight charges the railroads collected from other oil companies.

Obviously, few companies could compete successfully with Rockefeller's combination. When the arrangement was finally discovered, there was a howl from small businessmen and farmers. The farmers in particular had been victimized by the railroads, which charged them high rates to make up for losses on oil and other freight business.

Rockefeller and his associates quickly abandoned South Improvement and came up with the trust, a better plan for controlling the oil industry, in 1879. This plan called for the stockholders of forty oil companies to turn their stock (shares of ownership) over to nine men called trustees. In return the stockholders received certificates entitling them to collect dividends on their stock. The nine trustees (Rockefeller and his close associates), with full power over the forty oil companies, could undersell any competitor and drive it out of business.

Soon, many other trusts were formed—in meat packing, rubber, sugar, whiskey—as businessmen sought to protect themselves from competition and reap big profits. Again there were outraged howls from small businessmen who were threatened by the trusts. Consumers also feared that a trust, once it gained a monopoly over a product, would gouge them with high prices. They demanded action by Congress and the states.

Criticism of the trusts by the public and legislators brought angry retorts from big-business leaders. Joseph Wharton of Philadelphia declared, "I have supported the government more than it has supported and aided me. I am one of the men who create and maintain the prosperity of the nation and who enable it to survive even the affliction of wrong-headed and cranky legislators."

Commodore Vanderbilt of the New York Central was outraged when the state legislature passed a law to regulate his railroad. "Can't I do what I want with my own?" he asked. " 'Haint' I got the power?"

James J. Hill, another leader in the railroad business, insisted that the "fortunes of railroad companies are determined by the law of the survival of the fittest." Rockefeller agreed, but he put it a bit more poetically. "The growth of a large business is merely a survival of the fittest. . . . The American Beauty rose can be produced . . . only by sacrificing the early buds which grow around it. This is not an evil tendency in business. It is merely the working out of a law of nature and a law of God."

Needless to say, small oil companies, which found they were the buds to be sacrificed for Rockefeller's "American Beauty rose," were not charmed by his rhetoric.

In 1888 President Cleveland charged that corporations, "which should be the servants of the people," were "fast becoming the people's masters." That year both the Republican and Democratic parties called for a law to curb the trusts. In July, 1888, Senator John Sherman of Ohio introduced a resolution that led to the passage by Congress of the Sherman Antitrust Act in 1890. It declared illegal "every contract, combination in the form of trust or otherwise, or conspiracy in restraint of trade or commerce among the several states or with foreign nations."

Before the Sherman act was passed, the trusts had found a new and more effective way to set up large business combinations and control industries. A New Jersey law provided this new method in 1888. The law permitted one corporation to own the stock of another and holding companies were born.

Suppose a man had wanted to control forty sugar companies. It would have been costly, if not impossible, for him to buy a majority of the stock in all those companies. So instead the New Jersey law allowed him to get the owners of these companies to exchange shares of stock in their companies for shares in a newly formed holding

company. Then the man could sell shares of stock in the
holding company to the public. As this new business combination began to arouse public opposition, the famous
humorist Finley Peter Dunne had his favorite character
define a holding company. "It's when yu hand th' swag
to someone else while th' police search yu."

No one was sure whether or not the holding company
was legal under the Sherman act. But as months passed,
the government did not seem eager to enforce its antitrust
legislation. Furthermore, a series of Supreme Court decisions blocking state and federal attempts to regulate the
railroads gave big businesses the comfortable feeling that
all was right in their world of "free" competition.

State officials charged with regulating the railroads first
felt the firm hand of the Supreme Court in the *Railroad
Commission Cases* of 1886. The states had claimed the
right to regulate railroad rates in the interest of the public,
particularly the long-suffering farmers in the West. The
Supreme Court upheld state regulation of rates, but it
warned that rates must not be fixed so low that a railroad
could not make a reasonable profit. Cutting a railroad's
profit would violate the Fourteenth Amendment, which
prohibits the taking of private property without fair pay-
ment. This ruling was quite a jolt to the states, because it
meant that the Court had abandoned a position it had
taken a decade earlier.

In *Munn* v. *Illinois* in 1877, the Court had decided that
an Illinois law regulating the rates charged by grain ware-

houses did not deprive a corporation of its rights under the Fourteenth Amendment. Chief Justice Waite, who read the majority opinion, declared that private property was subject to government regulation when it was devoted to public use, as in the case of grain warehouses. The chief justice also pleased the states by saying that it was *not* the Court's job to make sure that the rates set by a state were reasonable. If rates were unjust, it was up to the people to elect a new legislature that would pass a law fair to all.

Waite's name was blessed by state officials, the farmers, and many newspaper editors, but there was a "joker" in his decision that few people paid any attention to at the time. In ruling that the Illinois law did not deprive a corporation of its rights under the Fourteenth Amendment, Waite for the first time said that the "person" mentioned in the amendment was a corporation as well as a human being.

For years big-business lawyers had been insisting that Congress had intended to treat corporations as persons when it wrote the due process clause of the Fourteenth Amendment. As shown in the *Slaughterhouse Cases* of 1873, Justice Miller rejected this argument. He said that the amendment was intended only to aid the newly freed slaves. But in 1877 Waite accepted the big-business definition that a corporation was a "legal person." But does calling a corporation a person make it a person? In his book, *This Honorable Court*, Leo Pfeffer recalls that

Lincoln once asked how many legs a dog would have if you called its tail a leg. "Five," was the answer. "No," said Lincoln, "calling a tail a leg does not make it a leg." But, adds Pfeffer, if the Supreme Court calls a corporation a person, it is a person—and that's that.

The Supreme Court played Waite's joker in the *Railroad Commission Cases* when it said that unfair rates— and the Court would itself decide what rates were unfair —violated a person's (corporation's) rights under the due process clause of the Fourteenth Amendment. Since "due process" is just about anything the Court says it is at the moment, there appeared to be no limit to the Court's power to knock out laws that a majority of the justices did not like. The Fourteenth Amendment, which had failed to protect the Negro, proved to be a stone wall of protection for business.

A few months later, in the case of the *Wabash, St. Louis and Pacific Railroad* v. *Illinois,* the Court used the interstate commerce clause of the Constitution to hamstring most state attempts to regulate railroads. In this case it ruled that a state cannot regulate a railroad within its own borders if that railroad is a part of interstate commerce—that is, if it runs from state to state. This decision denied states the power to regulate most of the big railroads since, as they usually ran across state lines, they clearly were a part of interstate commerce. And that could be regulated only by the federal government.

Angry farmers in the West hammered at Congress to

do something about the railroads. Four months after the *Wabash* decision, Congress passed the Interstate Commerce Act of 1887. This act established a federal agency, the Interstate Commerce Commission, to regulate railroad rates and forbid practices that might harm the public. But in the next few years, the railroads appealed sixteen cases involving the commission's attempts to regulate them and won fifteen.

Harlan went along with the Court majority on several railroad-regulation cases. He felt that the states, in trying to regulate the railroads, were getting into something that was the business of the federal government. He also followed the Constitution word for word, and he believed that it protected the life, liberty, *and* property of all, including railroads. But he just as strongly believed that the general welfare of the people was more important than property rights. Thus he contended that the federal government had the right under the Constitution to protect the people from illegal actions by the trusts. (The name "trust" was applied to any sort of business combination or holding company even after businessmen had been forced to abandon the trust method of controlling an industry.)

In 1895 the federal government finally decided to use the Sherman Antitrust Act. It sought to break up the sugar trust, which controlled ninety-eight percent of the sugar refining in the nation. But in the case, *United States v. E.C. Knight Company*, the Court voted eight-to-one

against the government. In his majority opinion, Chief
Justice Fuller said the Sherman act could be applied only
to interstate commerce. Then he took a very narrow view
of what interstate commerce actually was. He said it involved only the *movement* of goods from state to state,
not the *making* of goods in any one state. Fuller granted
that the manufacture of a product and the price charged
for it had some effect on the sale of it in other states. But
he contended that this effect was only "indirect." The
refining of sugar or the making of any other product was,
said Fuller, a local activity that could not be regulated by
the federal government.

In his dissent, Harlan angrily objected to the Court's
shrinking of the meaning of interstate commerce. He felt
that calling the refining of ninety-eight percent of the
nation's sugar a "local" activity was pure nonsense. He
warned that the great nationwide trusts were too powerful
to be regulated by the states. Only the federal government
could handle the job of protecting the people from
business practices which Harlan called "crimes against the
public."

A wave of public protest followed the decision in the
Knight case, and stronger actions were demanded against
the trusts. But Attorney General Richard Olney, the man
in charge of antitrust cases, shrugged off the uproar with
the comment: "The government has been defeated on
the trust question. I always supposed it would be, and I

have taken the responsibility of not prosecuting under a law I believe to be no good."

During the administrations of Harrison, Cleveland, and McKinley, the Sherman act was practically forgotten. Meanwhile, the leaders of industry and banking continued building more powerful business combinations. In 1900 the National Sugar Refining Company was organized, and in 1902 J. P. Morgan completed the formation of the United States Steel Corporation with a capital base of more than a billion dollars. United States Steel had enough money in its petty-cash box to have paid all the bills the United States government had in the year 1800.

19

★

Teddy Roosevelt
and the Trusts

When Theodore Roosevelt became president after the assassination of McKinley, he took a long look at the trusts and decided something had to be done. Roosevelt was especially annoyed at the Supreme Court's decisions favoring the railroads and other big businesses. "The President and Congress can say what they think they think," said Roosevelt, "but it rests with the Supreme Court to decide what they really have thought." This statement neatly summed up Harlan's attitude toward the Court. He felt that the Court majority was acting as a "super-legislature," rewriting by its decisions the laws that had been passed by Congress and state legislatures.

Looking over the Court membership in 1901, Roosevelt decided that he would get no help from Fuller, White, Peckham, or Brewer if he sought to regulate big business.

He was sure he could rely on Harlan. And he thought
McKenna, Brown, and Shiras might swing to the trust-
busting. In 1902 the death of Justice Gray gave Roosevelt
a chance to appoint a member of the Supreme Court. The
president wanted to appoint Oliver Wendell Holmes, Jr.,
son of the famous author and an outstanding legal scholar
and chief justice of the Supreme Judicial Court of Massachusetts. Before making the appointment, however, Roosevelt wanted to know what Holmes' attitude was toward
the trusts. Apparently assured of Holmes' liberal views,
Roosevelt appointed him. A year later, Justice Shiras resigned and Roosevelt appointed William R. Day of Ohio,
a judge of the federal circuit court of appeals. Day's
father, grandfather, and great-grandfather had all been
judges, and he himself had served as secretary of state in
McKinley's cabinet.

A battle for the control of a railroad empire gave Roosevelt a chance to see if there was any life left in the Sherman act. J. P. Morgan, who controlled the Northern
Pacific and other railroads, and his ally, James J. Hill
of the Great Northern, were challenged by E. H. Harriman of the Southern Pacific in 1901. At stake was control
of a railroad running into Chicago. After a fight that
had many businesses in an uproar, the three men finally
agreed to combine forces. They organized a holding
company called Northern Securities, which had a monopoly over rail transportation in the Northwest. Big
business was relieved by this settlement of the Morgan-

Harriman battle, and a majority of the people probably were not worried about the power of this new railroad combination. But Roosevelt felt the combination had to be broken up. He said that the "absolutely vital question" was whether the government had the power to control huge corporations. "It was necessary," he wrote later, "to reverse the Knight case in the interests of the people against monopoly and privilege, just as it had been necessary to reverse the Dred Scott decision in the interests of the people against slavery and privilege."

Roosevelt kept his plans secret. When Attorney General Philander Knox suddenly announced that the government intended to break up the Northern Securities combination, a startled and angry J. P. Morgan hurried to Washington. Acting as though he were doing Roosevelt a favor, the frosty-eyed Morgan said: "If we have done anything wrong, send your man [Attorney General Knox] to my man [one of his many lawyers] and they can fix it up." Annoyed by Morgan's attitude, Knox cut in bluntly: "We don't want to fix it up. We want to stop it."

Morgan's attorneys argued in Supreme Court that only New Jersey could regulate Northern Securities, which was a New Jersey corporation. They also contended that even though Northern Securities had a monopoly of transportation in the Northwest, this alone did not prove that the company intended to charge high rates and act in an illegal manner.

Eight years after he had dissented alone in the *Knight*

case, Harlan read the majority opinion of the Court in the *Northern Securities* case. Harlan brushed aside the company's attempt to use New Jersey as a refuge. He said Congress clearly had the power to regulate nationwide business combinations, and that the Sherman act forbade the "mere existence" of any combination that might restrain trade. Failure to break up Northern Securities, said Harlan, meant that "the entire commerce of the immense . . . part of the United States between the Great Lakes and the Pacific . . . will be at the mercy of a single holding corporation."

The Court was bitterly divided (five-to-four) on this case, and the makeup of the majority and minority surprised and angered Roosevelt. Brewer, whom the president had not counted on, joined Harlan, Brown, McKenna, and Day in supporting the government. Holmes, whom Roosevelt had counted on, joined the conservatives Fuller, White, and Peckham in opposing the government. Furthermore, Holmes added insult to injury by writing a salty dissent that accepted the arguments of Morgan's lawyers. Holmes contended that the fact that the merger of the Morgan-Hill-Harriman railroads had created a monopoly did not make it illegal. He insisted that "ferocious" competition by businessmen was more dangerous and harmful to the nation than a lack of competition.

As expected, Holmes' dissent brought an angry outburst from Roosevelt. "I could carve out of a banana a justice with more backbone than that!"

Justice Brewer, who had surprised everyone by voting with the majority, refused to go along with Harlan's far-reaching opinion. In a separate opinion Brewer said that the Sherman act was limited to preventing only "unreasonable restraints of trade." But he agreed that Northern Securities was an "unreasonable restraint." Harlan was glad to have Brewer's support, but he did not care for his opinion. He felt it was another case of a justice reading words into a law that Congress had not put there.

After his *Northern Securities* victory, Roosevelt followed the views of Brewer rather than those of Harlan. In fact, the president began saying that not all trusts were bad or would lead to "unreasonable restraints of trade." He did not kill the trusts; he just tried to tame them a bit. Roosevelt, who got the reputation of a "trust-buster," actually started far fewer suits against the trusts than President William H. Taft or President Woodrow Wilson. Even when trusts were broken up, the different companies found ways of working together. How do you unscramble a scrambled egg?

While the nation was grappling with the problems of controlling huge business combinations, the power of the federal government had suddenly spread to foreign lands. In 1898, the Spanish-American War resulted in annexation by the United States of Puerto Rico and the Philippine Islands. Most Americans were happy about the annexations, but the new possessions brought with them several tricky questions that bothered American officials.

For example, since Puerto Rico had become a territory of the United States, could Puerto Rican sugar enter the United States without paying a tax? The powerful sugar trust was, of course, opposed to the entry of low-cost Puerto Rican sugar. Or, since the Constitution guarantees trial by jury, did this mean that a Filipino criminal had to be tried by a jury composed of Filipinos? In short, did the Constitution follow the flag? American military men who were having trouble controlling the Filipinos snorted at the idea of granting a Filipino criminal a trial by jury.

In the case of *DeLima* v. *Bidwell*, decided in 1901 by a five-to-four vote, the Supreme Court ruled that, although Puerto Rico was no longer a foreign country, it still was not part of the United States. Therefore, Congress could enact laws imposing tariffs on Puerto Rican exports (particularly sugar). Harlan dissented strongly and refused to accept the idea that Puerto Rican goods could be taxed. Later he wrote a letter to Chief Justice Fuller: "The more I think of these questions, the more alarmed I am at the effect upon our institutions of the doctrine that this country may acquire territory inhabited by human beings anywhere upon the earth and govern it at the will of Congress and without regard to the restraints imposed by the Constitution upon governmental authority. There is a danger that commercialism will sweep away the safeguards of real freedom."

Three years later, as Harlan feared, the Court denied

an important safeguard of freedom to Filipinos. In the case of *Dorr* v. *United States* the Court, by an eight-to-one vote, denied a jury trial to a Filipino criminal, proving that the Constitution did not follow the flag. The majority opinion held that Filipinos could not claim the right of trial by jury unless Congress passed a law giving them that right. Dissenter Harlan protested that the decision placed Congress *over* the Constitution. He insisted that the Constitution was the "supreme law of the land" in every territory of the United States, and that the rights granted in the Constitution could not be denied to residents of these territories.

20

★

Still in
the Dissenting Business

In 1907 Harlan again fought vainly to bring to the citizen of a state the protection of the Bill of Rights. Thomas M. Patterson, publisher of the *Denver Times* and the *Rocky Mountain News*, wrote an article criticizing the judges of the state supreme court. For this he was held in contempt of court and faced imprisonment and a heavy fine. The Supreme Court turned down Patterson's appeal by a seven-to-two vote. Reading the majority opinion in *Patterson* v. *Colorado*, Justice Holmes held that the Fourteenth Amendment did not protect freedom of speech and press from action by a state.

Harlan's dissent, which was supported by Brewer, again hammered away on the rights that belong to every citizen. "I go further," he said, "and hold that the privilege of free speech and of free press . . . constitute essential parts

143

of every man's liberty, and are protected against violation by that clause of the Fourteenth Amendment forbidding a state to deprive any person of his liberty without due process of law. It is, I think, impossible to conceive of liberty, as secured by the Constitution against hostile action, whether by the nation or by the states, which does not embrace the right to enjoy free speech and the right to have a free press."

It would be years before the Court again faced the question of whether a person was deprived of liberty when a state took away the rights guaranteed him by the First Amendment. Finally, in *Gitlow* v. *New York*, 1925, the Court got around to deciding that the liberty in the due process clause of the Fourteenth Amendment included liberty of expression (free speech, free press).

In 1908, Harlan was to hear, to his anger, his own warnings against future attacks on a citizen's right to a fair trial turned against him by a Supreme Court majority. In *Twining* v. *New Jersey*, the Court, in an opinion by Justice Moody, declared that the Fourteenth Amendment did not prevent a state from forcing a person to incriminate himself. Harlan's earlier warning in the *Hurtado* case proved to be justified when Moody coolly said that, since the Court had previously ruled that grand-jury indictment was not a vital part of "due process," it was logical for the Court to allow the states "to compel any person to be a witness against himself." In his lone dissent, Harlan said, "I cannot support any judgment declaring that immunity from self-incrimination is not one of the privileges or immunities of national citizenship, nor a part of the liberty guaranteed by the Fourteenth Amendment against hostile state action." He quoted from seven state constitutions adopted between 1776 and 1784 which had clauses protecting persons from compulsory self-incrimination. Harlan held that "the wise men who laid the foundations of our constitutional government would have stood aghast at the suggestion that immunity from self-incrimination was not among the essential, fundamental principles of English law."

With evident relish, Harlan then backed up his argument by quoting from Justice Moody's own opinion. While warming up to the job of destroying the protection granted in the Fourteenth Amendment, Moody had said: "At the time of the formation of the Union, the principle that no person could be compelled to be a witness against himself had become embodied in the common law and [this principle] distinguished [common law] from all other systems of jurisprudence. It was generally regarded then, as now, as a privilege of great value, a protection to the innocent, though a shelter to the guilty, and a safeguard against heedless, unfounded or tyrannical persecutions."

In other words, Moody seemed to be saying that the protection against self-incrimination was "a privilege of great value." How then could it be *not* valuable enough to be given by New Jersey to a citizen of that state? Harlan, a man of great common sense, could see no logic in Moody's argument. He never got tired of reminding the Court majority that every man accused of a crime is presumed to be innocent until proven guilty. Thus, no man should be forced to give testimony against himself. That, to Harlan, was what the Fifth Amendment was all about.

21

★

The "Liberty"
to Work Ten Hours a Day

During the 1880's, the Supreme Court had ruled that corporations were persons entitled to the protection of the due process clause of the Fourteenth Amendment. Then in 1905, through the case of *Lochner v. New York*, the Court majority showed the nation how powerful this clause was as a weapon against state laws that business opposed. In 1897, the New York legislature passed a law prohibiting bakery workers from working more than ten hours a day or more than sixty hours a week. Joseph Lochner, the owner of a bakery in Utica, was fined $20 for requiring Frank Couverette to work more than sixty hours one week. For a second offense, Lochner was fined $50 or fifty days in jail. His case was heard by the Supreme Court in 1905.

In a five-to-four decision, the Court declared New

147

York's bakery law unconstitutional. Speaking for the majority, Justice Peckham called the law "unreasonable, unnecessary and arbitrary" and a violation of liberty under the due process clause of the Fourteenth Amendment. Laws of this kind, he said, were "mere meddlesome interferences" to keep "grown men" from taking care of themselves. A worker must be free to make his own contract with his employer. In denying New York the right to regulate hours of work in bakeries, Peckham announced that "the trade of a baker has never been regarded as an unhealthy one."

Both Harlan and Holmes wrote powerful dissents. Harlan answered Peckham's comment that "the trade of a baker has never been regarded as an unhealthy one." He cited the reports of health authorities to prove that "more than ten hours daily work each day, from week to week, in a bakery or a confectionery establishment, might endanger the health and shorten the lives of the workmen, thereby diminishing their physical and mental capacity to serve the state and to provide for those dependent upon them." Contending that an employee did not have equal bargaining power with his employer, Harlan said it was nonsensical to argue that a worker's "liberty" was taken away if the state limited his hours of work to protect his health. Again, Harlan criticized the majority for trying to take over the job of the state legislature by acting as a super-legislature.

"We are not to presume," Harlan said, "that the State

of New York acted in bad faith. Nor can we assume that
its legislature acted without due deliberation, or that it did
not determine the question upon the fullest attainable
information, and for the common good." Therefore, Harlan concluded, the Court had no good reason for knocking
out this law.

Harlan's carefully argued, fact-loaded opinion was brilliant, but not as often quoted as that of Holmes. Skillfully
handling Peckham's defense of a worker's liberty to work
as long as he likes, Holmes said: "I think that the word
liberty in the Fourteenth Amendment is perverted when
it can be held to prevent the natural outcome of a
dominant opinion, unless it can be said that a rational and
fair man necessarily would admit that the statute proposed
would infringe fundamental principles as they have been
understood by the traditions of our people and our law."
Thus Holmes agreed with Harlan that the Court should
not knock out the law unless the law violated constitutional rights and clearly had nothing to do with health or
safety.

Three years after Harlan's liberal dissent in the *Lochner*
case, pro-labor observers were startled by his opinion in
Adair v. *United States*. This case involved the Erdman
Act which had been passed by Congress in 1898 to regulate labor relations on the railroads and thereby seek to
avoid strikes. One part of the act made it a misdemeanor
for a railroad or any of its officials to fire a worker solely
because he had joined a union. Adair, a railway agent, was

convicted of violating this provision. By a six-to-two vote (Justice Moody was ill) the Court declared this part of the Erdman Act unconstitutional.

Harlan's majority opinion said the regulation in the Erdman Act was "an invasion of the personal liberty, as well as the right of property guaranteed by the Fourteenth Amendment." He said the *Adair* and *Lochner* cases differed because, in *Lochner*, there was a direct relationship between the hours of labor and the state's right to protect a worker's health. But in the *Adair* case, according to Harlan, there was no close relationship between Congress' power to regulate interstate commerce and the right of workers to join or not to join a union.

Holmes and McKenna dissented. Both argued that labor disputes could lead to strikes that could interfere with interstate commerce. Therefore, Congress had the power to regulate labor relations in order to prevent strikes. Holmes admitted being skeptical about the good that labor unions could do for workers, but he added that it was up to Congress to settle the matter, not the Court.

Harlan's distrust of business combinations may have influenced his attitude toward labor unions. In fact, in those days, the courts generally looked on a labor union as a "conspiracy" against the public. This attitude resulted in another costly defeat for unions only a short time after the *Adair* decision. In the *Danbury Hatters* case, the Supreme Court ruled *unanimously* that a union that tried to force a company to unionize its employees could be sued for damages under the Sherman Antitrust Act as a conspiracy in restraint of trade. Labor was outraged by this decision. It always had believed that the Sherman act applied only to business conspiracies. The act clearly states, though, that "every combination or conspiracy" is illegal, and it does not exempt unions. In the *Danbury Hatters* case, the union had sought to boycott a company (keep consumers from buying from the company) until it reached an agreement on unionization. This, said the Court, was clearly a "combination or conspiracy in restraint of trade." Labor leaders angrily pointed out that the Court was much more eager to convict a union than a trust, for it had ruled unanimously against the hatters' union, but was split five-to-four in the *Northern Securities* case. Years passed before Congress enacted a law specifically freeing unions from the restrictions of the Sherman act.

The year 1908 was a busy one for Harlan. The Kentuckian was back at his old stand, trying vainly to defend the rights of black citizens under the Fourteenth Amendment. The case involved Berea College, which had an enrollment of 174 black and 753 white students, and was the only college in Kentucky that admitted both whites and blacks. Berea was founded in the 1850's as an antislavery school to work among the non-slaveholding people of the hill country. The college was not just a trade school for mechanics or farmers. It also trained its students—black and white—to become lawyers, teachers, editors, architects. The black and white students studied and lived together in harmony, and there were several Negro teachers and board members at the college.

Berea's little island of racial sanity was attacked in 1904 by the Kentucky legislature. It passed a law making it illegal to operate a college or school "where persons of the white and Negro races are both received as pupils for instruction." The officials of Berea protested in vain against the law. When the college opened for the next academic year, all of Berea's black students were sent to Negro colleges. Setting an example of brotherhood and decency for state officials and legislators, Berea's white students sent the following message to the black students who had been exiled:

> . . . We realize that you are excluded from the class rooms of Berea College, which we so highly prize, by no fault of your own, and that this hardship is a part of a long line of deprivations under which you live. Because you were born in a race long oppressed and largely untaught and undeveloped, heartless people feel more free to do you wrong, and thoughtless people meet your attempts at self-improvement with indifference or scorn. Even good people sometimes fear to recognize your worth, or take your part in a neighborly way because of the violences and prejudices around us.
>
> We are glad to have known you, or known about you, and that we know you are rising above all discouragements, and showing a capacity and a character that give promise for your people. . . . We hope never to be afraid or ashamed

to show our approval of any colored person who has the character and worth of most of the colored students of Berea. We are glad that the college is providing funds to assist you in continuing your education, and we are sure the institution will find ways to do its full duty by the colored race.

Berea College lost its case in the Kentucky courts and so took it on to the Supreme Court. A Court majority upheld the Kentucky law as a proper regulation of a Kentucky corporation (Berea College) by the state. The decision in the *Berea* case was a heavy blow to Harlan. This school, in his home state, had been following the road to sane racial relations that he hoped the nation would someday follow. In his dissent, Harlan was furious because the Court had avoided the main question at issue: whether the legislature of a state may make it a crime for a private college to give instructions to both white and black students. Harlan firmly believed that the Kentucky law denied the rights of liberty and property guaranteed by the Fourteenth Amendment.

"Have we become so inoculated with prejudice," he asked, "that an American government, professedly based on the principles of freedom . . . can make distinctions between . . . citizens in the matter of their voluntarily meeting for innocent purposes, simply because of their respective races? Further, if the lower court is right, then a state may make it a crime for white and colored persons to frequent the same market places at the same time, or appear in an assemblage of citizens convened to consider questions of a public or political nature, in which all citizens, without regard to race, are equally interested. Many other illustrations might be given to show the mischievous, not to say cruel, character of the statute in question, and how inconsistent such legislation is with the great principle of the equality of citizens before the law."

In 1911, the last year of his life, Harlan was joined by a majority of the Court in blocking another attack on Negro rights. This case, *Bailey* v. *Alabama*, involved one of many laws Southern states had passed to get around the Thirteenth Amendment's ban on slavery. Lenze Bailey, an Alabama Negro, was found guilty in a state court of failing to carry out a contract to work for a year on a farm, and for not returning $15 he had been advanced at the time the contract was made. Under Alabama law, failure to complete the contract and return the money advanced was taken as evidence that the worker had intended all along not to work the required year. Furthermore, the law did not allow the defendant to swear under oath that he really had intended to carry out the contract when he made it. Caught in this legal trap for the unwary, Bailey was convicted and sentenced to 136 days at hard labor.

In 1883, over Harlan's strong objections, the Court had refused to use the Thirteenth Amendment in the *Civil Rights Cases*. Now, however, by a seven-to-two vote, the Court put some teeth in the Thirteenth Amendment. The majority opinion was written by Justice Charles Evans Hughes, who had recently joined the court. Hughes did not come right out and accuse Alabama of trying to enslave and oppress Negro workers, but did say that the law in question was peculiarly effective against the poor and the ignorant, its most likely victims.

It is most interesting to find Harlan, the ex-slaveholder, concurring with the majority, and Holmes, the three-times-wounded Union officer, dissenting. Furthermore, Holmes wrote an amazing opinion in which he argued that the Court's sympathy for a poor, ignorant black man should not prevent it from upholding the laws of Alabama.

22

★

Roar of an Angry Lion

Harlan's final dissent, and one of his most fierce, resulted from the government's antitrust action against Standard Oil. The Court ordered the company to be broken up. In its decision in May, 1911, the Court majority took the same position as Brewer had taken in his *Northern Securities* opinion. The Court held that the Standard Oil combination was illegal only because it was an "unreasonable restraint" of trade. Harlan approved the results of the *Standard Oil* decision, but he strongly objected to the principle on which it rested—the so-called "rule of reason."

In his dissent, Harlan sharply denounced the reading of the word "unreasonable" into the Sherman act, calling it a piece of judicial law-making. "The Court," Harlan thundered, "has now read into the act of Congress words which are not to be found there." The Sherman act, he

added, flatly declares illegal "every contract, combination or conspiracy in restraint of trade, not every *unreasonable* contract, combination or conspiracy." Harlan
then laid down a rule of behavior for federal judges.
"The courts have nothing to do with the wisdom or
policy of an act of Congress. Their duty is to ascertain
the will of Congress, and if the statute embodying the
expression of that will is constitutional, the courts must
respect it. They have no function to declare a public
policy, nor to amend legislative enactments." The rumble
and roar of Harlan's voice ceased. He sat down, and ob-
jects in the courtroom stopped vibrating. This was Harlan's final message from the Court to the American
people.

Justice Hughes later described Harlan's last dissent as
"no swan song, but the roar of an angry lion."

When the Supreme Court met for its new term on
October 9, 1911, Harlan was at his place on the bench.
As the senior justice, he was nearing his thirty-fourth
year of service. Still vigorous at seventy-eight, Harlan
could look forward to breaking the tenure record set by
Justice Field. The Court met for only one hour on that
opening day and then adjourned so the justices could
pay their respects, as was their custom, to the president.
Although ill, Harlan was present for the next two sessions
of the Court.

On October 13 he was reported to be suffering from
an acute attack of bronchitis. At 8:13 A.M., on October

14, 1911, Harlan died in his Washington home. His wife and four of his six children were at his bedside. President Taft, who was out of town, telegraphed his condolences to the family, and messages arrived from Theodore Roosevelt, William Jennings Bryan, and many other national leaders who had known Harlan personally or by reputation as a "famous constitutional authority." The funeral was held on October 17 at the New York Avenue Presbyterian Church and burial was in Rock Creek Cemetery, Washington, D.C. His tenure on the Court was exceeded only by those of Justice Field and Chief Justice Marshall.

All three of Harlan's sons were men of prominence in their chosen fields. Richard Davenport Harlan was a Presbyterian minister and president of Lake Forest College in Illinois. (John Marshall Harlan was himself a member of a Presbyterian church in Washington and conducted a Bible class there every Sunday until the final months of his life.) James Shanklin Harlan became a member of the Interstate Commerce Commission. John Maynard Harlan was a Chicago attorney and a member of the city's Board of Aldermen. (His son, named after John Marshall Harlan, is an associate justice of the United States Supreme Court.) One of the Harlans' three daughters, Edith Shanklin Harlan, married; and Laura and Ruth Harlan lived with their parents in Washington, D.C.

23
★
First of the
Modern Liberal Judges

Chief Justice Edward D. White, a Southerner who often opposed Harlan's stand on civil rights, complained that the Kentuckian "could lead but not follow." Other observers in Washington looked upon Harlan as an eccentric old fellow who made a business of dissenting. His ideas about the law were considered either old-fashioned or so far-out that they didn't make sense.

Harlan paid little attention to criticism, though. He was a practical person who applied the law in a common-sense way to the problems of his time. But he was far ahead of his time in demanding that the Fourteenth Amendment be used to give Negroes the "equal protection of the laws," and to guarantee all persons accused of crimes a fair trial. That is what a lot of Harlan's dissents were all about.

159

Harlan, the first of the great modern liberal judges, was in the dissenting business long before such liberals as Oliver Wendell Holmes and Louis D. Brandeis, and he was a more persistent dissenter than either. Holmes has often been called "the Great Dissenter," but Harlan actually has more claim to the title. During his thirty-three years, ten months, and twenty-five days on the Court, Harlan took part in deciding 14,226 cases. He delivered the majority opinion in 745 cases, and dissented in 380. Harlan participated in 39 cases dealing with the civil rights of blacks, and in every case in which the Court upheld the rights of Negroes, Harlan voted with the majority. In every case in which the Court declared federal civil rights legislation to be unconstitutional, he dissented. In every case in which the majority denied Negroes rights under the Thirteenth, Fourteenth, and Fifteenth Amendments, Harlan dissented. In a majority of all cases, Justice Harlan dissented alone.

Justice Charles Evans Hughes, who served on the Court from 1910 to 1916, later wrote a defense of the dissenting opinion:

"A dissent . . . is an appeal to the brooding spirit of the law, to the intelligence of a future day, when a later decision may possibly correct the error into which the dissenting justice believes the Court to have been betrayed."

Nearly a dozen of Harlan's most important dissents have become the law of the land. His appeal to "the brooding spirit of the law" has helped win for all Americans a large measure of protection from unfair treatment by the police and the courts. Dissenter Harlan argued steadily, often alone, that as a result of the Fourteenth Amendment (which forbade the states to deny due process to any person) the first eight amendments in the Bill of Rights applied to the states.

On June 23, 1969, in one of its final decisions under retiring Chief Justice Earl Warren, the Court virtually completed the task at which Harlan had worked vainly for years. In *Benton* v. *Maryland*, the Court held that the double jeopardy protection of the Bill of Rights applies to state as well as federal courts. And so today, eighty-five years after Harlan's dissent in the *Hurtado* case, only a few provisions of the Bill of Rights have yet to be applied to the state courts through the Fourteenth Amendment.

Recent decisions of the Court, strengthening the Fifth Amendment protection against self-incrimination, have brought demands that the Constitution be amended to give the police more power to obtain confessions from suspects. Harlan would have a blunt dissent for this. He would grant that in defending the rights of all, persons who don't deserve protection may be shielded from punishment. But he firmly believed that the rights of the best of men could be safeguarded only if the rights of the most unworthy of men were also protected.

Harlan's notable dissents in the *Civil Rights Cases*

and *Plessy* v. *Ferguson* gave clear warning of the racial strife to come, which the nation to its sorrow chose to ignore. Finally in 1954, in *Brown* v. *Board of Education*, the Court unanimously overruled *Plessy* v. *Ferguson*. "We conclude," said Chief Justice Warren, "that in the field of public education the doctrine of 'separate but equal' has no place. Separate educational facilities are inherently unequal. Therefore, we hold that plaintiffs . . . are by reason of the segregation complained of, deprived of the equal protection of the laws guaranteed by the Fourteenth Amendment."

Eighty-six years after it was written into the Fourteenth Amendment, the "equal protection" clause was used by the Court to put an end to the "separate but equal" doctrine. The next year, the Court ordered Southern states to desegregate their schools with "deliberate speed." However, the states proceeded with deliberate slowness. Then, in 1969, the Nixon administration asked the Supreme Court to allow a further delay in school desegregation in the South. But the Court, headed by Chief Justice Warren Burger, quickly ruled against the administration.

Two minor civil rights laws had been approved by Congress in the 1950's, but they did little to give blacks equality. In 1964, however, Congress passed the most sweeping civil rights act since the act of 1875. Within a few months, the Court unanimously upheld the desegregation of public accommodations section of the 1964 act. Harlan's dissent in the *Civil Rights Cases* had become the law of the land. Ironically, Harlan's grandson and namesake was a member of the Court that handed down this decision and the one in *Brown* v. *Board of Education.*

John Marshall Harlan had made brilliant contributions in the field of business regulation. His dissent in the sugar trust case later became the majority opinion of the Court in *Northern Securities Co.* v. *United States.* When the Court in the *Standard Oil Case* adopted the "rule of reason," Harlan dissented violently but in vain. The "rule of reason" became the rule of law in future antitrust cases, and so it remains today a controversial subject among legal scholars.

Business, labor, and farm leaders have mixed feelings about the Sherman Antitrust Act, but few people want to get rid of it. Businessmen believe both in competition and in protecting themselves from competition. This has kept the antitrust lawyers of the federal government busy. In 1969 they won a case against fifteen of the nation's largest makers of plumbing supplies. The companies were convicted of a conspiracy that "raised, fixed and stabilized" prices of bathtubs, sinks, and toilets. Damage claims totaling billions of dollars may have to be paid by the companies to purchasers of new homes who were overcharged while the price-rigging deal was in effect.

"The more costly such penalties prove," commented *The New York Times*, "the sooner companies in every branch of American industry will recognize that gouging consumers through price conspiracies is the antithesis of everything basic to an enterprise system. Until that realization, increased vigilance on the part of antitrust officials is a national necessity." This *Times* editorial sounds a lot like one of Harlan's warnings against the trusts back in the 1890's and 1900's.

John Marshall Harlan was a militant, fighting justice, and his most violent dissents generally involved cases in which he felt that the Court was reading words into a law that had not been put there by Congress or a state legislature. He believed that the Constitution was up-to-date enough to handle most problems faced by the nation. If the Constitution did not cover some new problem, it was the duty of the people, not the Supreme Court, to amend the Constitution. "No line of public policy," he declared, "can be long maintained in this country against the will of those who established, and can change, the Constitution."

In the past thirty years, the Supreme Court has given less attention to defending the property rights and more to protecting the liberties of the people, assuring to all the right to a fair trial. The sixteen-year record of the Court under Chief Justice Warren is especially notable.

In studying the 180-year history of the Supreme Court,

it is a cause for wonder that this group of men, not elected by the people and serving for life, has become the strongest defender of democracy and the rights of the people. John Marshall Harlan, whose courage, sympathy, and integrity shine through his hundreds of pages of judicial opinions, deserves much credit for the Supreme Court's towering reputation today.

Bibliography

*Recommended for further reading.

*Brant, Irving. *The Bill of Rights*. Indianapolis: Bobbs-Merrill, 1960. (For an excellent discussion of Harlan's defense of the Fourteenth Amendment see chapters 29 through 33.)

Clark, Floyd B. *The Constitutional Doctrines of Justice Harlan*. No. 4. Baltimore: Johns Hopkins Press, 1915.

Coulter, Ellis Merton. *The Civil War and Readjustment in Kentucky*. Chapel Hill: North Carolina Press, 1926.

Fairman, Charles. *Mr. Justice Miller and the Supreme Court, 1862-1890*. Cambridge: Harvard University Press, 1939.

Goff, John S. "Justice John Marshall Harlan of Kentucky." *Register of the Kentucky Historical Society*, 1960.

Hartz, Louis. "John M. Harlan in Kentucky." *The Filson Club History Quarterly* 14, 1940.

Hughes, Charles Evans. *The Supreme Court of the United States*. New York: Columbia University Press, 1936.

"John Marshall Harlan." *Dictionary of American Biography*. Vol. VIII, pp. 269-272.

McElroy, Robert M. *Kentucky in the Nation's History*. New York: Moffat, Yard and Co., 1909.

*Pfeffer, Leo. *This Honorable Court*. Boston: Beacon Press, 1965. (An outstanding study of the Court.)

Warren, Charles. *The Supreme Court in United States History*. Rev. ed. Boston: Little Brown, 1962.

Westin, Alan F. "John Marshall Harlan and the Constitutional Rights of Negroes: The Transformation of a Southerner." *The Yale Law Journal* 66, April, 1957. (The author is indebted to Dr. Westin for making available a copy of *The Yale Law Journal* containing his most valuable article. No full-length biography of Harlan has been published, and I eagerly await Dr. Westin's forthcoming book on a giant of the Court who has too long been neglected by historians.)

Index

169

Harris, Isham, 23
Harrison, Benjamin, 85
Hayes, Rutherford B., 69, 70, 71
Hill, James J., 128, 137
Holmes, Oliver Wendell: appointment to the Court, 137; dissenting opinions, 139, 148-149, 150, 155, 160; regard for Harlan, 114
Holt, Joseph, 19-20, 33
Home Guard, 22-23
Howe, Timothy O., 71
Hughes, Charles Evans, 75, 155, 157, 160
Hunt, Ward, 81, 82, 83
Hurtado v. *California*, 102-104

Immigrants, 10, 11
Imperialism, legal problems posed by United States policy, 140-142
Income tax case, 108-112; Harlan's dissent, 109-111
Indictment by a grand jury. *See* Due process of law; Fifth Amendment; Trial by jury
Ingersoll, Robert, 91
Interstate commerce: definition, 132, 134; Interstate Commerce Commission, 133; regulation of, 104

Jackson, Andrew, 1-2
Jackson, Howell E., 85-86, 111
Jacob, Richard, 37, 50
Jim Crow, 96, 122. *See also* Racial discrimination
Johnson, Andrew, 45, 47, 49, 54-55
Joint Committee on Reconstruction (Committee of Fifteen), 47

Judicial review, 77. *See also* Supreme Court
Judiciary Act of 1789, 74

Kansas-Nebraska Act, 10
Kentucky: attitude on slavery and emancipation, 31, 33-34, 56; postwar problems, 50, 52, 61-68; role in Civil War, 20-26, 30, 41-42. *See also* Harlan, John Marshall: party affiliation of
Kentucky Presbyterian Church, 58
Knight Company, E. C. *See United States* v. *E. C. Knight Company*
Know-Nothing party, 10-11, 12, 13
Knox, Philander, 138
Ku Klux Klan, 56
Ku Klux Klan Act, 60

Labor, 96, 147-51. *See also* Business: government regulation of; Sherman Antitrust Act
Lamar, Lucius Quintus Cincinnatus, 84, 85
Lee, Robert E., 43, 46
Leslie, Preston B., 58-59, 63, 66
Lincoln, Abraham: attitude toward Kentucky, 23, 25, 42; election as president, 17; plans for emancipation, 30-34, 40; Reconstruction plan, 44; speaks out against Kansas-Nebraska Act, 10
Lochner v. *New York*, 147-149; Harlan's dissent, 148-149
Louisiana: railroad law, 119-121, 123, *Slaughterhouse Cases*, 100-101; withdrawal of federal troops, 70-71
Louisville streetcar crisis, 64-65

)81

n Marshall Harlan, 1833–1911
t ed.₁ New York, Cowles Book

ı. 4.95

ᴅɪᴜ

1. I.